WordPerfect

A READY REFERENCE MANUAL

CATHERINE GARRISON

MERCEDES A. McGOWEN

MARILYN K. POPYK

ADDISON-WESLEY PUBLISHING COMPANY, INC.
Reading, Massachusetts • Menlo Park, California • Don Mills, Ontario
Wokingham, England • Amsterdam • Sydney • Singapore • Tokyo
Madrid • Bogotá • Santiago • San Juan

This book was produced by Addison-Wesley using MicroTEX. The output was generated on an Apple Laser Writer.

The procedures and applications presented in this book have been included for their instructional value. They have been tested with care but are not guaranteed for any particular purpose. The publisher does not offer any warranties or representations, nor does it accept any liabilities with respect to the programs or applications.

First Printing, February 1987
Reprinted with corrections September, 1987.

Copyright ©1987 by Addison-Wesley Publishing Company, Inc.

All rights reserved. No part of this publication may be reproduced, stored in a retrieval system, or transmitted, in any form or by any means, electronic, mechanical, photocopying, recording, or otherwise, without the prior written permission of the publisher. Printed in the United States of America. Published simultaneously in Canada.

ISBN 0-201-11626-x WordPerfect: A Ready Reference Manual
    EFGHIJ-AL-8987

Introduction

Why purchase this book? Because you will learn to use WordPerfect faster if you can look up the action that you wish to perform. For about the price of a fast-food dinner for two, you can own a convenient summary of WordPerfect procedures. Long after dinner would be digested, the Ready Reference Manual will still be there to assist you.

Want to know a little more about the Ready Reference Manual? It is a convenient summary of commonly used WordPerfect procedures and commands. It is designed to assist you in performing common word processing tasks, such as inserting a word or deleting a line.

Unlike most manuals, this one is organized by function, rather than by command. This enables you to find the action that you need to perform without knowing the specific commands used in the procedure.

Like most manuals, this one is intended act as a reference tool. For a complete introduction to and definition of word processing concepts, you should read the word processing chapters in Marilyn Popyk's *Up and Running! Microcomputer Applications* before beginning to use WordPerfect.

IMPORTANT INSTRUCTIONS FOR USERS OF THE ENHANCED EDUCATIONAL VERSION

An enhanced educational version of WordPerfect 4.2 is available to users of Marilyn Popyk's *Up and Running! Microcomputer Applications.* This version of WordPerfect will permit you to do almost everything that you could do with the regular version of WordPerfect. However, you should know the following facts about the enhanced educational version:

1. Saved documents are limited in size to approximately 50,000 characters. This is approximately 25–30 regular pages of text.
2. "*WPC" will be printed after each paragraph as a disclaimer.
3. Advanced printing features are not allowed.
4. LPT1 (PRN) is the only port that can be used for printing. The Printer Selection option of the Print menu is disabled on the educational disk. This means that you cannot use this menu to select a printer.
5. The Help function is not active. When Help is requested, a template is displayed showing the WordPerfect activities that are assigned to each function key.
6. One will be able to learn all the functions of WordPerfect 4.2's speller and thesaurus by calling up the "readme.wp" file and following the step-by-step directions. However, there are only a limited number of words in the speller and thesaurus, and they cannot be used effectively with created documents.

Differences from the regular version of WordPerfect are marked in this manual with a multiplication sign (×).

WordPerfect
CORPORATION

School Software Direct Order Form
Provided by Addison-Wesley

Qualifying teachers, as well as college, university, and other post-secondary students can now purchase WordPerfect Corporation (WPCORP) software directly from WPCORP at a reduced price. To qualify, a participant must be teaching or currently enrolled as a full-time student, and must agree in writing not to resell or transfer any package purchased under this program.

If you satisfy these conditions and would like to purchase software directly from WPCORP under the School Software Program, complete the following seven steps and sign at the bottom of the form.

Step 1   From the list below, select the appropriate software for your computer (please note that each student is limited to *one* package of WordPerfect) and mark an "x" in the corresponding box(es).

Product	Disk Size	Computer	Price*
☐ WordPerfect 4.2	5 1/4"	(IBM PC/XT/AT/Compatibles)	$125.00
☐ WordPerfect 4.2	3 1/2"	(IBM PC/XT/AT/Compatibles)	125.00
☐ WordPerfect 1.1	5 1/4"	(Apple IIe/IIc)	59.00
☐ WordPerfect 1.1	3 1/2"	(Apple IIGS)	59.00
☐ MathPlan 3.0	5 1/4"	(IBM PC/XT/AT/Compatibles)	99.00
☐ WordPerfect Library	5 1/4"	(IBM PC/XT/AT/Compatibles)	59.00
☐ WordPerfect Library	3 1/2"	(IBM PC/XT/AT/Compatibles)	59.00

Step 2   Make a photo-copy of your current Student ID card or Faculty card *and* a photo-copy of some well known form of identification displaying your social security number, such as your Driver License or Social Security Card. (WPCORP will hold this information strictly confidential and use it only to guard against duplicate purchases.) If you do not want to provide WPCORP with a social security number, you must provide alternative *verifiable* information sufficient to protect against duplicate purchases.

Step 3   Enter your social security number: _____ - __ - _____ .

Step 4 Enclose payment for the total cost of the package(s) ordered with personal check, money order, Visa or MasterCard.

Account # _____

Expiration Date _____ ☐ Visa ☐ MasterCard

(Make check or money order payable to WordPerfect Corporation.)

Step 5 List your shipping address in the space provided:

Ship to _____

_____

_____

Phone _____

Step 6 Address a stamped envelope to School Software Program, WordPerfect Corporation, 288 West Center Street, Orem, UT 84057.

Step 7 Enclose this signed and completed form, the photo-copies of your identification cards, and your signed check or money order (or Visa or MasterCard account number and expiration date) in the envelope and seal it securely. Then mail it.

The information provided herein is correct and accurate, and I will abide by the restricting conditions outlined by WPCORP in this document. I understand that at its sole discretion, WPCORP may refuse any order for any reason.

Signature _____ Date _____

*Utah residents add 5.75% sales tax.

WordPerfect Corporation, 288 West Center Street, Orem, Utah 84057

Contents

INTRODUCTION TO WORDPERFECT   1

An Overview of WordPerfect   1
The Keys   2
    Function Key Assignments   4
Function Summary by Action   6

ENTERING AND EXITING WORDPERFECT   9

Loading WordPerfect   9
The Screen   10
    Interpreting the Status Line   10
Entering Text   11
Moving the Cursor   11
    Horizontal Movement through the Text   11
    Vertical Movement through the Text   12
Entering Dates   12
Changing the Date Format   12
Entering Text That is to be Aligned at the Right Margin   13
Aligning/Pushing Existing Text to the Right Margin   13
Restoring Text   13
Canceling a Command   14
Repeating a Command or Character   14
Requesting Help   15

Revealing the Screen Symbols   15
    Interpreting the Screen Symbols   16
    Changing the Screen Symbols   17
Clearing the Screen with Option to Abandon the Document   17
Saving a Document and Resuming Work   18
    Selecting the Drive That Will Contain the Document   18
Saving/Replacing an Existing Document   19
Leaving WordPerfect   19

FORMATTING A DOCUMENT   21

Using Default Formats   21
Changing the Page Format   22
Changing the Line Format   22
Setting Margins   22
    Changing the Top Margin   22
    Changing the Bottom Margin/Paper Size   22
    Changing the Left and Right Margins   24
Changing the Right Margin Justification   25
Changing Line Spacing   26
Using Tabs and Decimal Tabs   26
    Displaying the Tab Options   26
    Setting the Tab Alignment Character   28
Automatically Reformatting a Document   28
    Turning Automatic Formatting/Rewrite Off   28
    Reformatting/Rewriting Text   28
Printing Page Numbers Automatically   29
Changing the Page Number   29
Suppressing Page Numbers, Headers and Footers   29
Using Headers and Footers   30
    Creating Headers or Footers   30
    Printing Different Headers or Footers
      on Alternate Pages   32
    Discontinuing a Header or Footer   33
    Changing the Text of a Header or Footer   33
    Changing the Margins on a Header or Footer   33
Using Footnotes   34
    Creating Footnotes   34
    Editing Footnotes   35
    Changing the Footnote Number   35
    Changing Footnote Margins   35
    Deleting a Footnote   36

ENTERING AND EDITING TEXT 37

- Using Word Wrap   37
- Using Hyphenation   38
  - Types of Hyphens   38
  - Turning Hyphenation On   38
  - Adjusting the Hyphenation Zone   39
  - Inserting a Hyphen in a Word   40
  - Removing a Hyphen   40
  - Turning Hyphenation Off   41
- Hyphenating Phrases   41
- Entering Dashes   41
- Entering a Minus Sign   41
- Centering Text on the Page   41
- Centering Text on a Line   42
- Centering Blocks of Text   42
- Going to a Tab and Entering Text   42
  - Going to a Tab and Aligning Numbers or Text with a Value   43
- Indenting Paragraphs   43
- Undoing Indentation for One or More Lines of Text   43
- Indenting the Left and Right Margins of a Paragraph   44
- Inserting Text   44
- Typing Over Text   44
- Inserting Extra Blank Lines   44
- Deleting a Character   44
- Deleting a Word   45
- Deleting to the End of Line   45
- Deleting a Blank Line   45
- Deleting to the End of Page   45
- Deleting a Page Break   45
- Deleting a Code   45
- Copying or Moving a Sentence, Paragraph or Page   46
- Manipulating Blocks of Text (Copying, Moving, Deleting)   46
  - Using Highlighting when Identifying Blocks of Text   47
  - Defining a Block of Text   47
  - Canceling Highlighting   47
  - Displaying a Block of Text   47
- Deleting A Block of Text   48
- Copying Text within a Document   48
- Copying Text From One Document into Another   48
  - Inserting an Existing Document into Another   48
  - Moving or Copying a Column   49
- Moving a Block of Text   50
- Creating Newspaper and Parallel Columns   50
  - Defining Newspaper Columns   50

Defining Parallel Columns   51
   Building Columns   52
Editing Newspaper and Parallel Columns   52
Locating Information/Global Searches   53
   Finding a Word or Pattern of Characters   53
Replacing Information   54
   Replacing Items in a Block   54
   Replacing All or Just Some Items   55
   Deleting Every Occurrence of An Item   55
Adjusting the Amount of Text on a Page/Pagination   55
   Forcing a Page Break   55
   Keeping Text Together/Conditional Page Break   56
   Preventing a Page Break within a Block of Text   56

CREATING SPECIAL TEXT EFFECTS   57

Creating Bold Text   57
   Entering Bold Text   57
   Changing Existing Text to Bold Text   58
Using Subscripts and Superscripts   58
Underlining Text   59
   Selecting an Underlining Style   59
   Underlining Text as You Type   60
   Stopping Automatic Text Underlining   60
   Underlining Existing Text   60
Removing Unwanted Underlining   61
   Revealing the Code and then Removing It   61
   Removing Underlining without Revealing Codes   61

PRINTING   63

Printing a Document   63
   Printing the Current Document   63
   Printing a Portion of a Document   64
   Printing a Document Stored on Disk   64
   Printing More Than One Document   65
   Printing Multiple Copies of a Document   65
   Stopping a Print Job   66
   Resume Printing a Job That Has Been Stopped Previously   66
   Canceling a Print Job   66
   Printing a Job Out of Sequence (Rush Print Job Option)   67
   Displaying All Print Jobs Waiting   67
Typewriter Mode   67
   Line by Line Type-thru   68

Correcting Typing Mistakes before Printing 68
Clearing Characters from the Screen 68
Temporarily Installing a Printer 69
Changing Printers 69

THE SPELLING CHECKER AND THE THESAURUS 71

Using the Spelling Checker 71
Checking the Spelling in a Document 72
    Correcting Double Word Occurrences 73
The Thesaurus 73
    Looking Up a Word Contained in a Document 73
    Using the Thesaurus 74
    Moving a Displayed Column of Synonyms Up or Down 75
    Replacing the Word in the Document with a Selected Word 75
    Looking through the Document for Other Words 75
    Looking Up a Word Not Contained on a Displayed List 76
    Erasing the Columns 76

WORKING WITH MULTIPLE DOCUMENTS 77

Using Windows and Screens 77
Switching Between Two Documents 77
Transferring Text Between Two Documents 78
Splitting the Screen/Windows 79
    Opening a Window 79
    Viewing the Same Document in Two Windows 79
    Moving Between Windows 81
    Closing a Window 81

CREATING FORM DOCUMENTS 83

Form Letters and Templates 83
    Merge Documents 83
    Master Documents 83
    Keeping Track of Master Documents 84
Using Templates to Customize a Letter 84
    Inserting Commonly Used Phrases into a Document 84
    Creating Customized Documents from a Master Document 85
Using the Merge Facility 86
    Merge Codes 87
    Entering Merge Codes 89
    Creating a Primary Document 89

ix

    Creating a Data File/Secondary Document   91
    Creating a File That Prompts for Information to Be Merged   92
    Merging a Form Letter and a Data File   93
    Merging a Form Letter with Keyboard Information   94
    Merging to the Printer   95
    Stopping a Merge   95
    Restarting a Merge   95
    Printing Mailing Labels   95
    Linking Several Documents or Templates Together   96
Sorting Information   97
    Selecting The Sort Function   97
    Sorting a Block of Text   98
    Using the Sort/Select Display to Describe the Sort   98

DOCUMENT FILING AND HOUSEKEEPING   101

The Document Directory   101
Accessing or Changing the Directory   101
    Locating a Document Name   101
    Leaving the Document Directory   102
Copying a Document   103
Deleting a Document   103
Browsing/Looking at a Document   104
Locating Documents That Contain Specific Words   104
Printing a Document   105
Renaming A Document   105
Retrieving a Document from the Directory   106
Retrieving a Non-WordPerfect Document from the Directory   106
Translating Documents to and from ASCII   106
    Using the Text-In/Out Function to Translate Documents   107
Converting Documents into other Formats   107
Backing Up Documents   108
Restoring a Backup Document   109

DEFAULTS   111

The Set-Up Menu   111
Using the Set-Up Menu   111
    Setting the Automatic Backup Using the Set-Up Menu   112
    Installing the Backup Features   112
    Changing Formatting Defaults Permanently   113
    Changing Screen Size   114

Changing Drives and/or Directories for Speller
    and Thesaurus   114
Invoking Automatic Backup When Starting WordPerfect   114
Invoking WordPerfect Without the Fast Option/Adjusting
    WordPerfect for TopView and DeskTop Packages   114

Introduction to WordPerfect

AN OVERVIEW OF WORDPERFECT

WordPerfect is a word processor that permits you to create and edit document more rapidly than using a typewriter. It is one of the first word processors to fully take advantage of a hard disk system. It handles directories and subdirectories with ease and provides rapid ways of searching through a long list of document names. If you are using the complete non-educational version on a system that does not have a hard disk, it is strongly recommended that you ask someone to set up a RAM disk in memory for you.

When you enter WordPerfect, you will see an empty screen. You may either begin entering the document that you wish to create or retrieve an existing document and make changes to it. Function keys are used to tell WordPerfect what action you wish to perform. A document is stored in memory until it is saved. When you save a document, it is written to disk. You assign a name to a document at the time it is saved. If you specify the name of an existing document, the document will be replaced.

To see a list of existing documents, press F5 and enter the name of the directory which you wish to view. WordPerfect will then display a list of all of the documents in a directory. Unlike some word processors, WordPerfect lets you use the PgUp and PgDn keys to move through the directory a screen at a time. Procedures are provided that let you search for a file name or to list all of the files that contain a particular word or phrase. You can perform most file management functions, such as copying, renaming, or deleting files from this directory.

THE KEYS

To communicate with WordPerfect, you press a key or a combination of keys on the computer keyboard. The keyboard consists of several types of keys:

Typewriter Keys or character keys are used to enter text. For example, A B C 1 2 3.

The Numeric Key Pad also contains a key for each of the digits 0 through 9. The Numeric Key pad is often positioned just to the right of the typewriter keys. Pressing NUM LOCK activates this keypad. (On the IBM keyboard, NUM LOCK is the grey key immediately above the keypad.) When the key pad is activated, *Pos* flashes in the bottom right corner of the screen.

Warning: Do NOT use the numbers on this keypad when responding to WordPerfect prompts. Instead use the numbers in the first row of the typewriter keys.

The Numeric Key pad also contains keys that can be used use to move the cursor. So it might also be called a Cursor Movement Key pad.

The Cursor Movement Keys Are:

- The Up arrow (↑) moves the cursor toward the top of the screen.
- The Down arrow (↓) moves the cursor toward the bottom of the screen.
- The Right Arrow (→) moves the cursor to the right.
- The Left Arrow (←) moves the cursor to the left.
- The Home key modifies the meaning of other cursor movement keys.
- The End key moves the cursor to the end of the line.
- The Minus (−) key moves the cursor up one screen.
- The Plus key (+) moves the cursor down one screen.
- The INS key switches you from Insert mode to Typeover mode. In Insert mode, the characters that you type are inserted at the cursor position and the text is pushed to the right. In Typeover mode, the typed characters replace the characters at the current cursor position. When you enter WordPerfect, you are in Insert Mode.
- The DEL key deletes the character at the current cursor position. When used immediately after a block command, it erases a block of text.
- The Backspace key (←——) deletes the character to the left of the cursor.

Note: Not all keyboards contain a numeric key pad. In that case, the cursor movement characters are often located to the right and left of the typewriter keys.

Function Keys are identified by the letter F followed by a number, e.g., F1. There are ten function keys numbered F1 through F10. On some keyboards, these keys appear above the typewriter keys. On other keyboards, they are located to the left of the typewriter keys. Each of these keys performs a specific task or activity. For example, pressing F10 causes a document to be saved. You may modify the activity assigned to a function key by pressing the SHIFT, ALT, or CTRL key. For example, holding down the SHIFT key and pressing F10 causes WordPerfect to retrieve a file from storage. Holding down CTRL and pressing F10 causes WordPerfect to remember a series of keystrokes.

Transaction Keys interrupt processing, change processing modes, or send text to the computer's storage area. The transaction keys are:

SHIFT	changes the case of a letter from lower case to upper case. When two characters are printed on a typewriter key, pressing SHIFT causes the upper character to be printed. For example, holding down SHIFT and pressing 0 types a right parenthesis. The SHIFT key also can be used to modify the meaning of a function key.
CAPS LOCK	is used when you need to type a string of upper case letters. Pressing it once causes the letters to be typed in upper case. Pressing it again returns you to lower case mode. Unlike many typewriters, pressing CAPS LOCK does not affect any of the other keys. For example, if you press 0, 0 will be typed. You must still press the SHIFT key to type a right parenthesis.
ENTER RETURN	tells the computer that you have finished entering text. You should press RETURN at the end of each paragraph. When responding to WordPerfect prompts, you do not need to press enter after one letter responses such as Y for YES or N for No, since WordPerfect is expecting only one letter. However, when you are entering longer responses, such as the name of a file, you must press ENTER to indicate that your response is completed.
BACKSPACE	deletes the character one space to the left of the current cursor position.
TAB	moves the cursor to the next tab stop.
ESC	repeats a key or function.

The SHIFT, ALT, and CTRL Keys modify the meaning of other keys. They are usually positioned to the left of the typewriter keys. These keys are most commonly used to assign a new meaning to each function keys. When using these keys, press the modifier key and then press the function key once.

Caution: Tap the function key once, do not hold it down for several seconds. If you press the key too long, either the computer will beep to indicate that you have made an error or the function will execute more than once.

Function Key Assignments

When the function key is pressed, the activities listed below will be performed.

Actions Caused by Pressing a Function Key

Key	Meaning
F1	Cancel the last command. It is also used to recover deleted text.
F2	Search forward for a word, code, or tab.
F3	Request Help
F4	Indent the text
F5	List the files in the directory
F6	Turn Bold (dark) type on or off
F7	Exit WordPerfect
F8	Turn Underlining on or off
F9	Used to separate the fields to be merged
F10	Save the document and resume work

Functions Accessed by Holding Down the SHIFT Key

Key	Meaning
F1	Superscript or subscript text
F2	Search backward through the document
F3	Switch the text in the block from upper to lower case or from lower to upper case
F4	Indent text
F5	Insert the current date in the text. Also used to change the format of the date
F6	Center text
F7	Print a page or a document, or use the printer as a typewriter
F8	Display line formatting options
F9	Used to separate the records to be merged
F10	Retrieve a document

Functions Accessed by Holding Down the CTRL Key

Key	Meaning
F1	Shell / DOS access
F2	Spell checker
F3	Screen rewrite, line drawing, colors
F4	Move or copy text
F5	Read a non-WordPerfect document in or write it out
F6	Tab align
F7	Create or edit a footnote
F8	Select options that determine the appearance of the document at print time, such as margin justification
F9	Merge or sort information
F10	Define macros

Functions Controlled by the ALT Key

Key	Meaning
F1	Thesaurus
F2	Replace text
F3	Reveal WordPerfect codes
F4	Define a block of information
F5	Mark text for outline, index, redline, etc.
F6	Flush right
F7	Turn math or columns on
F8	Select page formatting characteristics
F9	Display merge codes
F10	Name / start macro to be used

FUNCTION SUMMARY BY ACTION

Action to Be Performed	Key
Block	ALT and F4
Bold text	F6
Cancel the last command	F1
Center text on line	SHIFT and F6
Center page on page	ALT and F8
Colors	CTRL and F3
Convert document	CONVERT (from DOS)
Date insertion, formats	SHIFT and F5
Display template	F3, F3
Exit WordPerfect	F7
File management functions	F5
Flush right	ALT and F6
Footnotes	CTRL and F7
Headers and footers	ALT and F8
Help	F3
Hyphenation	SHIFT and F8
Indent text	F4
Justification	CTRL and F8
Line drawing	CTRL and F3
Line menu	SHIFT and F8
List documents in directory	F5
Macro definition	CTRL and F10
Macro execution	ALT and F10
Margin justification	CTRL and F8
Margin setting—left and right	SHIFT and F8
Margin setting—top and bottom	ALT and F8
Mark text for outline, index	ALT and F5
Merge or sort records	CTRL and F9
Merge codes	ALT and F9
Mark merge field	F9
Mark merge record	SHIFT and F9
Math columns	ALT and F7
Move or copy text	CTRL and F4
Outline	ALT and F5

Action to Be Performed	Key
Page formatting	ALT and F8
Page numbering	ALT and F8
Pagination: conditional	ALT and F8
Print a document or page	SHIFT and F7
Print pitch or font	CTRL and F8
Redline text	ALT and F5
Return to DOS temporarily	CTRL and F1
Replace text	ALT and F2
Retrieve (paste) text	CTRL and F4
Retrieve a document	SHIFT and F10
Reveal codes	ALT and F3
Save a document	F10
Screen rewrite	CTRL and F3
Search forwards	F2
Search backwards	SHIFT and F2
Spacing	SHIFT and F8
Spelling checker	CTRL and F2
Superscript or subscript text	SHIFT and F1
Switch the text case	SHIFT and F3
Tab setting/clearing	SHIFT and F8
Tab align	CTRL and F6
Thesaurus	ALT and F1
Translate documents into WordPerfect	CTRL and F5
Translate document into ASCII	CTRL and F5
Typewriter mode	SHIFT and F7
Underlining off or on	F8
Underline style	CTRL and F8
Undelete the last erasure	F1, 1
View list of documents in directory	F5

Entering and Exiting WordPerfect

LOADING WORDPERFECT

This procedure assumes that WordPerfect has been installed.

1. Insert the operating system in disk drive A and turn on the computer. (This boots the system.)
2. If prompted for the time and date, either enter RETURN to use the time and date shown or enter new values.
3. When the operating system prompt A> appears, remove the disk containing the operating system and insert the disk containing WordPerfect.
4. In disk drive B, insert the document file disk. This may be:
   - a blank formatted disk
   - a disk containing existing files to be edited
   - a disk on which you wish to store new output
5. Type B: to make B the default drive; press RETURN.
6. Type A:wp and press RETURN.
7. Press the spacebar.
8. If a screen containing instructions appears, read the screen, and then press RETURN.

   Users of the educational version will see an additional screen that describes some of the product limitations. Press RETURN when the screen has been read.

A blank screen will appear. A status line will be displayed in the lower right corner. It shows the document, page, line and column number of the current cursor location.

Note: This procedure assumes that your copy of WordPerfect has been initialized for the type of printer most commonly used at your installation. Use the procedure called *Temporarily Installing a Printer* in the *Printing* chapter if you wish to change the printer assignment.

THE SCREEN

When you enter WordPerfect, you will see a blank screen. You may either fill this screen with new text or fill it with an existing document by retrieving the desired file.

The **cursor** will be displayed in the upper right corner. This is a blinking underline or rectangle that indicates your current position on the screen. When you type text, it will be inserted at the current cursor location.

Interpreting the Status Line

When you enter WordPerfect, the status line is the last line on the screen. Your current position in the document is displayed in the bottom right corner of the screen. Messages from WordPerfect are also displayed on this line.

The first part of the status line shows the number of the document you are working on. When you enter WordPerfect, you will always be working on document 1 (Doc 1). You may use the screen command to switch to a second document if desired. Normally, however, you will want to work on document 1.

Next the status line shows the number of the current page (Pg).
Third, it shows the current line number (Ln).
Finally, the current position number (Pos) is displayed. Note:

- If CAPS LOCK is on, the Pos is displayed in all upper case letters (Pos).
- If underlining is on, the position number will be underlined (Pos $\underline{n}$).
- If NUM LOCK is on, Pos will blink to indicate that the key pad is in numeric mode.
- If bold is on, the position number will be in boldface.

ENTERING TEXT

To enter text, simply press the desired keys. The text will be inserted on the page at the current cursor location. When the cursor reaches the end of a line, it will automatically proceed to the next line. The words being entered will also wrap around to the next line. This is called **word wrap**. The text on each line will be right justified at print time, unless you change the print options to indicate that you want a ragged right edge.

Caution: Do NOT press the RETURN key at the end of each line. You should press RETURN only at the end of a paragraph or when you want to insert an extra line. If you press RETURN at the end of each line, WordPerfect cannot automatically adjust the line spacing when you make changes to the text.

If you wish to change a section of text, use the arrow keys to position the cursor on the text to be changed, and then insert the desired changes. When you move the cursor to the next line, the text will be adjusted so that it fits within the specified margins.

When you reach the end of a paragraph you should press RETURN twice. The first RETURN marks the end of a paragraph. The second RETURN inserts a blank line between paragraphs.

MOVING THE CURSOR

Movement through the document is accomplished by using the arrow keys to move the cursor or by pressing a combination of keys. Note: When entering a combination of keys separated by the word AND, hold down the first key and tap the second key .once. For example, to move one word to the right, hold down the CTRL key and press the right arrow.

When entering a combination of keys separated by commas, tap each key in the sequence in which it is listed. For example, to go to the beginning of the text, press HOME twice, then press the up arrow.

Horizontal Movement through the Text

To Move:	Press:
One letter to the right	The right arrow (→)
One letter to the left	The left arrow (←)
One word to the right	CTRL and right arrow
One word to the left	CTRL and left arrow
Beginning of line	HOME and left arrow or END and right arrow
End of line	END

Vertical Movement through the Text

To Move:	Press:
Up one line	The up arrow (↑)
Down one line	The down arrow (↓)
Up one screen	Minus sign (−) or HOME and down arrow
Down one screen	Plus sign (+) or HOME and down arrow
Up one page	PgUp
Down one page	PgDn
Beginning of text	HOME, HOME, up arrow
End of text	HOME, HOME, down arrow
Go to a page	CTRL and HOME, page number, RETURN
Go to character	CTRL and HOME, character, RETURN
Go to beginning block	CTRL and HOME, ALT and F4
Go to beginning page	CTRL and HOME, up arrow
Go to end page	CTRL and HOME, down arrow

ENTERING DATES

1. Insert the cursor at the location where you wish the date inserted.
2. Hold down SHIFT and press F5 to display the date menu at the bottom of the screen.

   This list of options will appear: *Date 1 Insert Text; 2 Format; 3 Insert Function:0*

3. Press 1 to insert the current date.

   Note: This is the date that was entered when the system was booted or the Date command issued. If the computer has an internal battery-driven clock-calendar, the date will be taken from it.

   Note: Instead of a 1, press a 3 to update the date whenever the document is retrieved or printed.

CHANGING THE DATE FORMAT

The date may contain up to 29 characters, including punctuation and spaces.

1. Hold down SHIFT and press F5 to display the date menu.
2. Press 2 to change the format the date is displayed in.

A list of options for formatting the date is displayed. Immediately below this list, the combination of options currently in effect is highlighted. For example 3 1, 4 indicates that the name of the month will be displayed followed by a numeric day and then a four digit year; for example, October 8, 1987.

3. Enter 2 to display a numeric value when the month is displayed. Otherwise, enter a 3 to display the name of the month.

   Note: To display the day first, instead of the month (30 October), enter 1 or 6 to indicate the day format to be used, numeric or word.

4. Enter a comma, slash, space, or any other punctuation that is desired.
5. Enter the number opposite the day format that you wish to use.
6. Enter a space, comma, slash, or any other punctuation desired.
7. Enter the number opposite the year format that you wish to use.

ENTERING TEXT THAT IS TO BE ALIGNED AT THE RIGHT MARGIN

Dates and addresses are often aligned on the right margin. Use this command to enter the text at the current cursor location and then flush or push it to the right margin.

1. Hold down ALT and press F6 once.

   The cursor will move to the right margin.

2. Type the text to be aligned at the right margin.
3. Press RETURN.

ALIGNING/PUSHING EXISTING TEXT TO THE RIGHT MARGIN

Use this procedure to push existing text to the right margin.

1. Position the cursor in front of the text to be pushed to the right margin.
2. Hold down ALT and press F6 once.

RESTORING TEXT

WordPerfect saves the last three "chunks" of text that you deleted. You may recover any of the three chunks by using the procedure below to display the text to be restored and then insert it at the current cursor location.

Note: If a command is active, you must either cancel or finish the command before you can recover the desired text.

1. Press F1 to select the Cancel/Undelete function.

    The last text that you deleted will be highlighted and displayed at the current cursor location. Also, this message will appear at the bottom of the screen: *Undelete 1 Restore; 2 Show Previous Deletion: 0*

2. Press 1 to restore the highlighted text.

    Press 2 to see the previous text that was deleted.

    If no text has been deleted, then no text is displayed. A small blank "window" may be highlighted on the screen.

3. Repeat step 2 until you have displayed and selected the block of text to be restored.

CANCELING A COMMAND

This procedure works for most WordPerfect commands. However, it should not be used to cancel macro definitions. They are canceled by holding down CTRL and pressing F10 (the Macro Def key).

1. Press F1.

    You will be returned to the previous prompt. If there is no prompt, you will be returned to the document.

2. Repeat step 1 until you have returned to the desired starting point.

REPEATING A COMMAND OR CHARACTER

Characters are repeated when you wish to create a pattern by filling a line with the same character, for example, to separate two sections of a document by a line of dashes. Commands are repeated when you wish to execute the same command more than once.

Note: Another way to repeat the value on a key is to hold the key down until the desired number of characters have been typed. (Some commands may also be repeated by using the same technique.)

1. Press ESC

    This will be displayed: *n=* followed by a number.

2. Enter the number of times that the command is to be repeated. For example, press 2 to repeat the command twice.

Do NOT press RETURN.

3. Enter the key combination representing the command or character that is to be repeated. To continue the above example: press = to insert two equal signs at the current cursor location.
4. Press RETURN to activate the command or F1 to cancel it.

REQUESTING HELP

× This function is not available to users of the educational disk. Instead, when Help is requested, a template is displayed that shows the activities assigned to each function key.

Note: Hard disk users may omit the first two steps and the last two steps.

1. Remove the data diskette from drive B:.
2. Insert the Learning diskette into drive B:.
3. Press F3.
4. Press any letter key to see a list of functions.

   Alternative: Press the key combination that represents the function that you wish information on. For example, press F1 to see information on the Cancel command.

5. Press the letter representing the function on which you desire more information.

   Alternative: You can press the function key itself instead of the letter representing the function, if you wish.

6. Press the spacebar or RETURN when you are ready to leave HELP.
7. Remove the Learning diskette.
8. Insert the data diskette.

REVEALING THE SCREEN SYMBOLS

WordPerfect inserts symbols in the text to tell it when to place text in boldface, indent, center a line, end a line, etc. You may display these symbols and, if desired, change them.

1. Hold down ALT and press F3.

   The Format line will be displayed immediately below the current cursor location. It will be highlighted. A left brace ({) indicates the position of the left margin. Arrows indicate the position of the tabs. A right bracket

15

(|) indicates the location of the right margin.

Note: The format line divides the screen into two parts. If no text has been entered, one cursor will blink at the first position on the screen above the format line. Another will blink at the first position after the format line. If text has been entered, the text surrounding the current cursor location will appear at the top of the screen. (Since there is not room for all the text, the three lines above and below the cursor line are selected for display.) The status line is displayed below the last line of text. Next the format line is displayed. Then a copy of the text appears below, with the WordPerfect processing codes displayed.

2. Press RETURN when you wish to hide the codes again.

Interpreting the Screen Symbols

WordPerfect uses codes to tell it how to format a document when it is printed. Codes may be changed by typing over them or by pressing the backspace key to delete them. A list of the most commonly used codes follows.

CODE	Meaning
[◊] (blinking)	Current cursor position
[ ]	Hard space (always prints)
[-]	Hard hyphen (always prints)
- (blinking)	Soft hyphen (prints only when needed)
/ (blinking)	Cancel hyphenation
[A][a]	Begin or end tab alignment or flush right
[B][b]	Begin or end bold text
[Block]	Beginning of a block
[BlockPro:Off]	Block protection off
[BlockPro:On]	Block protection on
[C][c]	Begin or end centering
[Center Pg]	Center page top to bottom
[CndlEOP:n]	Conditional end of page: number of lines
[Col Def]	Column definition
[Col Off]	End text columns
[Col On]	Begin text columns
[Date: n]	Date/time
[EInd]	End of indent
[Font Change:n,n]	Font change
[Hdr/Ftr:n,n;text]	Header or footer definition
[HPg]	Hard page
[HRt]	Hard return (always ends line)
[Hyph on]	Hyphenation on
[Hyph off]	Hyphenation off

16

CODE	Meaning
[→ Indent]	Beginning of indent
[→ Indent ←]	Beginning of left/right indent
[LPI:n]	Lines per inch
[Margin Set:n,n]	Left and right margin reset
[Ovrstk]	Overstrike preceding character
[Pg#:n]	New page number
[Page# Col:n,n,n]	Column position of page number
[RedLn][r]	Begin and end redline
[RtJustOff]	Right justification off
[RtJustOn]	Right justification on
[SPg]	Soft new page (breaks if needed)
[SRt]	Soft return (creates new line if needed)
[StkOut][s]	Begin and end strikeout
[SubScrpt]	Subscript
[SuprScrpt]	Superscript
[Suppress:n]	Suppress page format options
[TAB]	Move to next tab stop
[Tab Set:]	Tab reset
[TopMar:n]	Top margin
[U][u]	Begin and end underlining
[W/O Off]	Widow/orphan off
[W/O On]	Widow/orphan on

Changing the Screen Symbols

1. Press INS to place WordPerfect in typeover mode if you wish to type over the symbols.
2. Hold down the ALT key and press F3 to reveal the codes.

   The Format line will be displayed immediately below the current cursor location. A copy of the original text will be displayed below the format line. The screen symbols will be displayed in the copied text. A complete list of symbols is shown above.
3. Use the arrow keys to position the cursor on the symbol to be changed.
4. Type the desired symbol, or press the delete (DEL) or backspace key to remove a symbol.
5. Press RETURN when you wish to hide the codes again.

CLEARING THE SCREEN WITH OPTION TO ABANDON THE DOCUMENT

When you are done using a document, you should clear or erase the screen.

This erases the document currently in memory and permits you to begin work on a new document.

1. Press F7.
2. Enter Y if you wish to save the document.

   If you do not save the document, any changes made to the document since the last SAVE instruction will be erased.

3. Enter the name of the document to be saved or press RETURN to use the displayed name if you have already assigned a name to the document.
4. Enter N to stay in WordPerfect.

SAVING A DOCUMENT AND RESUMING WORK

Warning: To prevent the loss of work that you have completed, save your document every few pages or after a set number of minutes. See *Setting the Automatic Backup* in the *Defaults* chapter if you wish to have WordPerfect automatically back up the document.

1. Press F10 to select the Save function.
2. Enter the name of the document to be saved.

   • The document name can consist of any combination of eight letters and numbers, except that it should not begin with a number. If desired, you may add a file extension to the end of the name by entering a period and a three character code. Common file extensions are: .doc .dat .wrk.

   Note: If you have saved the document before, the name of the document will be displayed. See *Saving/Replacing an Existing Document* below for instructions.

3. Press RETURN.

Selecting the Drive That Will Contain the Document

1. Press F10.
2. Enter the drive that is to contain the document.
3. Enter a colon (:).
4. If you are using a hard disk, enter the path to get to the document, for example, \ account.
5. Enter the name to be assigned to the document when it is saved.
6. Press RETURN.

SAVING/REPLACING AN EXISTING DOCUMENT

If a document name already exists in the directory, WordPerfect will ask whether you wish to replace the document. This helps protect you from accidentally overlaying a document with the wrong text.

1. Press F10.

    The name of the document will be displayed.

2. Press RETURN.

    The prompt *REPLACE filename? (Y/N): N* will appear.

3. Enter the name to be assigned to the document when it is saved, or press Y to replace an earlier version of a document with the new version.

4. Press RETURN.

LEAVING WORDPERFECT

1. Press F7.

    The prompt *Save Document? (Y/N): Y* will appear.

2. Press Y or RETURN to save the document displayed on the screen; otherwise, press N and proceed to step 5 to erase all changes made since the last save was performed.

    The name of the document will be displayed.

3. Press RETURN.

    The prompt *REPLACE filename? (Y/N): N* will appear.

4. Enter Y or a new document name.

    The prompt *Exit WordPerfect? (Y/N): N* will appear.

5. Press Y to Exit WordPerfect.

Formatting a Document

USING DEFAULT FORMATS

Since most people create documents that resemble a typewritten page in size, WordPerfect automatically will adjust your text to fit on a standard $8 \frac{1}{2}$ by 11 inch page with one inch margins. These values are called **default** values because WordPerfect defaults to or uses them without being told. If desired, you may change these values with others of your own. The default values WordPerfect uses to format your document are as follows:

- Page length — 66 lines (6 lines per inch)
- Lines per page — 54
- Page width — 80 columns
- Left margin — 10 (first column on the screen)
- Tabs — Every 5 characters
- Right margin — 75 (one inch)
- Number of characters per line — 65
- Pitch — Pica (10 characters per inch)
- Justification — Even right edge
- Top margin — 6 lines (one inch)
- Bottom margin — 6 lines (one inch)
- Page numbers — None
- Page number columns — Left 10, Center 42, Right 74
- Underlining — Non-continuous single
- Alignment character — Period

CHANGING THE PAGE FORMAT

The Page Format menu is displayed when you hold down the ALT key and press F8. It controls the location of the page number, the page number that is printed, page centering, the length of the page, the number of text lines on the page, the top margin, headers and footers, and what text will be kept on the same page.

CHANGING THE LINE FORMAT

The Line Format menu is displayed when you hold down the SHIFT key and press F8. It controls the line spacing, margins, tab placement, the tab alignment character, and hyphenation.

SETTING MARGINS

Once margins are set, you can center text horizontally or vertically by using the procedure *Centering Text* in the *Entering and Editing Text* chapter. The top margin formatting command takes effect at the current cursor location.

Changing the Top Margin

The top margin is defined in half lines rather than full lines. Two half lines make up one line of spacing. This provides you with greater spacing flexibility.

1. Hold down the ALT key and press F8 to display the Page Format menu.
2. Type 5 to select *Top Margin*.

    The prompt *Set half lines (12/inch) from 12 to:* where *from 12* represents the current top margin setting.

3. Determine the number of lines needed by multiplying the desired margin size by the number of half lines that will print in one inch. (The default is 12.)

    For example, to create a 1 1/2 inch margin, multiply 1.5 by 12. The result is 18.

4. Press RETURN to return to the Page Format menu.
5. Press RETURN to return to the document.

Changing the Bottom Margin/Paper Size

The bottom margin is calculated by (1) adding the number of lines in the top margin and the number of lines allocated for text and then (2) subtracting that total from the number of lines on each page.

Note: You may change margin size or page length at any point in a document. To change it for the entire document, position the cursor at the beginning of the document before beginning this procedure.

1. Hold down the ALT key and press F8 to display the Page Format menu.
2. Type 4 to select Page Length.

   Three Paper options and the current Paper setting will be displayed. The three options are:

   - Letter Size Paper should be selected if you (a) are using $8\frac{1}{2}$ by 11 size paper and (b) need one-inch top and bottom margins. This option creates a page with 66 lines on it, 54 of which are reserved for text. This is the default setting.
   - Legal Size Paper should be selected if you are (a) using $8\frac{1}{2}$ by 14 size paper and (b) need one inch top and bottom margins. This option creates a page with 84 lines on it, 72 of which are reserved for text.
   - Other (Maximum Length 108 Lines) should be selected if you are using nonstandard paper or margins. If you are not using one-inch top or bottom margins, you must use this option to indicate the number of lines of text that are to be printed on the page.

3. Press the number opposite the paper size that you need to use. For example, if you are using $8\frac{1}{2}$ by 11 inch forms with three-inch margins, press 3 for Other.

   Note: If option 1 or 2 is entered, you will be returned to the Page Format menu. You may then press RETURN to leave the menu. Otherwise, if option 3 was entered, proceed to the next step.

Defining Nonstandard Forms or Margins (Option 3)

The cursor will be positioned on the total number of lines on the form. The default is 66.

4. Enter the total number of lines that could fit on the page if the top and bottom margins were zero.
5. Press RETURN.

   The cursor will move to the number of lines that are actually available for text entry. The default is 54.

You must now determine how many text lines will fit on a page. This is done by deciding what size bottom margin is required, adding the size of the top and bottom margins, and then subtracting the result from the number of lines that will fit on a page. The following steps describe how to do this.

6. Calculate the bottom margin size by multiplying the desired bottom margin size by the lines that print in an inch.

    For example, to create a $1\frac{1}{2}$ inch bottom margin on a page that uses Pica type (6 lines per inch), multiply 1.5 by 6. The result is 9.0 lines.

7. Calculate the total number of lines used by the top and bottom margins by adding the result of step 6 to the number of lines in the top margin.

    For example, if both the top and bottom margin are $1\frac{1}{2}$ inches, the total number of lines used by the margins is 9 plus 9 or 18.

8. Determine the total number of lines of text that will fit on the page by subtracting the result of step 7 from the total number of lines in the page.

    The result is the number of lines available for text entry.

9. Enter the result of step 8 at the cursor position immediately after the prompt: *Number of single spaced text lines.*
10. Press RETURN to return to the Page Format menu.
11. Press RETURN to leave the Page Format menu.

Changing the Left and Right Margins

Use this procedure to (1) adjust the margin size when the size of the paper or the pitch changes or (2) vary the standard margin settings of one inch.

Note: The right margin is represented on the Format line as a right bracket (]). To change it for the entire document, position the cursor at the beginning of the document before beginning this procedure.

1. Hold down the SHIFT key and press F8 to display the Line Format menu.

    Note: The menu will appear at the bottom of the screen.

2. Type 3 to select the Margins.

    The prompt *Margin Set 10 74 to Left =* will be displayed. The first number, 10 in this example, represents the current left margin setting. The next number represents the current right margin setting; 74 is the default.

3. Determine the margin size by multiplying the margin width by the number of characters that print per inch.

    Note: When using Pica font (the default), approximately 10 characters print in one inch.

    For example, to set a $1\frac{1}{2}$ inch left margin, multiply 1.5 by 10. The result is 15.

Note: If you are setting one-inch margins, as a general rule you may use the pitch as the new left margin setting.

4. Type the desired left margin.
5. Press RETURN.

   The prompt *Right =* will appear.

6. Determine the new right margin by using one of the formulas below.

   To create a one inch right margin, multiply the pitch by 7.5 and subtract 1.

   For example, Pica type prints 10 characters per inch. 10 x 7.5 is 75, less 1 is 74. This is the WordPerfect default.

   To allow for fractions of an inch, determine how many characters will print in the fraction of an inch, and adjust the margin accordingly.

   For example, if you are using Pica type and need to set the right margin at $1\frac{1}{2}$ inches, you would:

   a) Determine what a one-inch margin would be (74).

   b) Determine how many characters would print in the fraction of an inch. In this case, 5 characters will print in $\frac{1}{2}$ inch.

   c) Subtract the result of step b from the result of step a. For example, $74 - 5 = 69$. This is the new right margin setting.

7. Enter the new right margin setting.
8. Press RETURN to return to the document.

CHANGING THE RIGHT MARGIN JUSTIFICATION

When you initially enter WordPerfect, the right margin will be **justified** when it is printed. This means that extra spaces will be inserted in the text so that the right margin appears to be even. If you prefer to print pages with a *ragged* or uneven right edge, you must turn justification off.

Note: A ragged right edge will appear on the screen even if justification is turned on. The text is justified when it is printed.

1. Position the cursor at the location where the new margin justification is to begin.
2. Hold down CTRL and press F8 to see the Print Options menu.
3. Type 3 to turn Right justification OFF; this will cause a ragged right edge to be printed.

OFF will appear opposite the option.

Type 4 to turn Right justification ON.

ON will appear opposite the option.

You will be returned to the Print Options menu.

4. Press RETURN to return to the document.

CHANGING LINE SPACING

1. Hold down the SHIFT key and press F8 to display the Line Format menu.

   Note: The menu will appear at the bottom of the screen

2. Type 4 to select Spacing.

   Spacing Set 1 (or the number that the current line spacing is set at) is displayed.

3. Enter the desired line spacing.

   For example, entering a 2 will double-space lines.

   Note: To skip half a line, enter .5. For example, .5 causes the printer to skip one-half a line before it prints the next. 2.5 skips two and a half lines before printing.

   Note: Enter nothing to retain the current line spacing.

4. Press RETURN to save the line number and return to the document.

USING TABS AND DECIMAL TABS

A tab marks a position in a document that can be returned to by pressing the TAB or Indent key.

To align text on a character, such as a decimal point, press the Tab Align key (CTRL and F6) instead of Tab.

Displaying the Tab Options

Before you can modify the tab settings, you must use this procedure to display the current tab settings and the menu of tab options.

1. Hold down the SHIFT key and press F8 to see the Line Format menu.

   Note: The menu will appear at the bottom of the screen.

2. Type 1 to see the Tab options.

   A ruler line showing the existing tabs is displayed along with a menu of tab options.

3. If desired, modify the tabs using one of the procedures that follows.
4. Press F7 to exit the menu.

Clearing and Resetting All Tabs

The following steps will delete all tabs and then place tabs at a specified interval throughout the format line. To modify selected tabs, see the following procedures.

1. Display the Tab options using the procedure above.
2. Hold down the CTRL key and press the END key to erase all tabs.
3. Enter the number of the column where the first tab is to be placed.
4. Enter a comma.
5. Enter the number of spaces between tabs.
6. Press RETURN to set the tabs.
7. Press F7 to exit the option menu.

Selectively Adding a Tab

1. Display the Tab options using the first procedure in this section.
2. Enter the number of the column where the tab is to be inserted; press RETURN.
3. (Version 4.2 Only) Justify the text associated with the tab by typing one of the options below and then pressing RETURN. If no option is entered, the text will be left justified.

   C centers text;   L left justifys it;
   R right justifies it   D aligns it on decimal
   . (period) automatically inserts a bullet at the tab location.

4. Repeat steps 2 and 3 to set another tab or press F7.

Selectively Deleting Tab Settings

1. Display the Tab options by using the first procedure in this section.
2. Enter the column number of the tab you need to delete; press RETURN.

   Note: The cursor will be positioned on the tab.

3. Press the DEL key to delete the tab.

4. Repeat steps 2 and 3 to delete another tab or press F7.

Setting the Tab Alignment Character

It is often desirable to align text on a particular character. For example, numbers are usually aligned on a decimal point; lists of names are often aligned on the space between the first and last name; formulas are aligned on slashes. WordPerfect permits you to align text on any character. The character may be changed within the document as many times as desired.

To advance to the tab align character press CTRL and F6.

1. Hold down SHIFT and press F8 to see the Line Format menu.

   Note: The menu will appear at the bottom of the screen.

2. Type 6 to see the Tab Alignment Character.

   The prompt *Align Char =* is displayed on the status line.

3. Enter the character that is to trigger text alignment.

AUTOMATICALLY REFORMATTING A DOCUMENT

When you make editing changes and Automatic Rewrite is on, WordPerfect automatically adjusts text to fit the margin and page specifications. If you are making extensive changes to a document, or if you are working with multiple documents or newspaper columns, you may wish to turn this feature off. You can then manually adjust the text when desired by pressing CTRL and F3 twice.

Turning Automatic Formatting/Rewrite Off

1. Hold down CTRL and tap F3 to see the Screen menu.

   A menu of screen control options appears in the prompt line.

2. Type 5 to select *Auto Rewrite*.

   The prompt *Auto Rewrite (Y/N)* will appear.

3. Enter N to turn the rewrite feature off.

Reformatting/Rewriting Text

If Rewrite is off, text must be manually reformatted after it is edited by using this procedure.

1. Hold down CTRL and press F3 to select the Screen menu.

    Note: The menu will appear at the bottom of the screen.

2. Press 0 or repeat step 1 to rewrite the text.

PRINTING PAGE NUMBERS AUTOMATICALLY

Once you specify the location where the page number is to be printed, Word-Perfect will automatically print page numbers.

1. Position the cursor at the location where page numbering should begin.
2. Hold down the ALT key and press F8 to display the Page Format menu.
3. Type 1 to select *Page Number Position*.

    A list of page number locations will be displayed.

4. Press the number opposite the location where the page number is to print.

    For example, pressing 3 causes the page number to be printed in the top right corner of each page in column 74.

5. Press RETURN to leave the Page Format menu.

CHANGING THE PAGE NUMBER

This procedure starts page numbering at the specified number.

1. Hold down the ALT key and press F8 to display the Page Format menu.
2. Type 2 to select New Page Number.

    New Page # is displayed.

3. Enter the desired starting page number.

    Note: Do not enter anything if you wish to retain the displayed starting page number.

4. Press RETURN to save the page number.
5. Press RETURN to leave the Page Format menu.

SUPPRESSING PAGE NUMBERS, HEADERS, AND FOOTERS

Use this procedure if you would like to omit page numbers, headers or footers from the current page.

29

1. Hold down the ALT key and press F8 to display the Page Format menu.
2. Type 8 to see a menu of options that can be suppressed on the current page.

   Note: A list of the options that can be suppressed is displayed.

3. Enter the number of the first option to be suppressed.

   For example, type 2 to turn page numbering off.

4. To suppress more options, enter a plus sign +, then enter the number of the next option that you need to suppress.

   For example, enter 2 + 5 to suppress page numbers and to suppress Header A.

5. Repeat step 4 until you have listed each item that you need to suppress.
6. Press RETURN to save your changes.
7. Press RETURN to leave the Page Format menu.

USING HEADERS AND FOOTERS

Headers print at the top of each page. Footers print at the bottom. Headers and Footers will not appear on the screen unless you are editing them or looking at revealed codes.

Once a header or footer is entered, it is automatically printed at the appropriate place on the page until you enter another header or footer. Space for headers and footers should be included in the number of available text lines when you modify the page length. WordPerfect automatically leaves a blank line between the header and the main text. One line is left between the text and the footer. The first line of the footers is printed on the last line in the page. The remaining lines of the footer are printed in the margin.

Two different headers and two different footers can be in use at any given time. You can print both headers or both footers on the same page or, if you wish, you can specify one header or footer for the right pages, and another for left pages. If you print two headers on the same page, be sure that they are on different lines or they may overlap.

You may change or discontinue a header or footer at any time.

Note: If you choose to print the page number in the header or footer, be sure to turn regular page numbering off. This may be done by selecting option 1 (Page Position) on the Page menu and then selecting the No Page Number option.

Creating Headers or Footers

Repeat this procedure once for each header or footer to be created.

1. When inserting the header on a page that contains text:

   a) Position the cursor at the top of the first page that is to contain the header or footer.

   b) Hold down the ALT key and press F3 to reveal codes.

   c) Move the cursor to the right until it is positioned next to the first hard return code.

   Note: This gives the header or footer the same margins as the rest of the document.

2. Hold down the ALT key and press F8 to display the Page Format menu.
3. Type 6 to select *Headers or Footers* options.

   Note: The Header and Footer Specifications options are displayed on the screen. These options control when the header or footer is printed.

4. Enter the number representing the type of title you need to create.

   - Type a 1 or a 2 to create a header.

   - Press a 3 or 4 to create a footer.

   Note: Header A, Header B, Footer A and Footer B have no special meaning. They are simply names that can be used to differentiate one header or footer from another.

   The cursor will move to the Occurrence frequency.

5. Enter when the header or footer should print.

   The options are:

   - Press 0 to discontinue the header or footer.

   - Type 1 to print the header or footer on every page.

   - Type 2 to print it on odd pages.

   - Type 3 to print it on even pages.

   - Type 4 to edit an existing header.

   A blank screen will appear.

6. Enter the text to be printed in the header or footer.

   Note: The text will appear exactly as it is entered, so be sure that it is formatted properly. Use the appropriate function or cursor movement keys to center, bold, underline or otherwise format the text.

7. To print the page number in the header or footer:

   a) Position the cursor at the location where the page number should appear and

   b) Hold down the CTRL key and press B.

8. Press F7 to return to the Page Menu.
9. Repeat the above steps to define another header or footer or press RETURN to return to the document.

Printing Different Headers or Footers on Alternate Pages

1. Hold down the ALT key and press F8 to display the Page Format menu.
2. Type 6 to select *Headers or Footers* options.

   Note: The Header and Footer Specifications options are displayed on the screen. These options control when the header or footer is printed.

3. Enter 1 to create the first header or 3 to create the first footer.

   Note: In the future, to refer to this header, select the Header A or Footer A option, as appropriate.

   The cursor will move to the Occurrence frequency.

4. Type 2 to print the header or footer on odd pages.

   A blank screen will appear.

5. Enter the text to be printed in the header or footer.
6. To print the page number in the header or footer:

   a) Position the cursor at the location where the number is to print, and

   b) Hold down the CTRL key and press B.

7. Press F7 to return to the Page Menu.
8. Type 6 to select *Headers and Footers*.
9. Enter 2 to create the second header or 4 to create the second footer.

   Note: In the future, to refer to this header, select Header B or Footer B option, as appropriate.

   The cursor will move to the Occurrence frequency.

10. Enter 3 to print the header or footer on even pages.

    A blank screen will appear.

11. Enter the text to be printed in the header or footer.
12. Refer to step 6 for instructions if you need to print the page number in the header or footer.
13. Press F7 to return to the Page Menu.
14. Press RETURN to return to the document.

Discontinuing a Header or Footer

1. Hold down the ALT key and press F8 to display the Page Format menu.
2. Type 6 to select *Headers or Footers* options.

   Note: The Header and Footer Specifications options are displayed on the screen.

3. Enter the number opposite the name of the header or footer to be discontinued.

   The cursor will move to the Occurrence frequency.

4. Enter 0 to discontinue the header or footer.
5. Press RETURN to leave the Page Format Menu.

Changing the Text of a Header or Footer

1. Position the cursor after the header or footer code in the text.

   If necessary, hold down the ALT key and press F3 to reveal the codes.

2. Hold down the ALT key and press F8 to display the Page Format menu.
3. Type 6 to select *Headers or Footers* options.

   Note: The Header and Footer Specifications options are displayed on the screen.

4. Press the number opposite the name of the header or footer that you need to edit.
5. Type 4 to edit the header.
6. Make the desired changes to the text.
7. Press F7 to save your changes and exit.
8. Press RETURN to leave the Page Format menu.

Changing the Margins on a Header or Footer

Warning: If the document margins are changed after a header is created, the header must be edited if you wish it to have the same margins as the text.

1. Hold down the ALT key and press F8 to display the Page Format menu.
2. Type 6 to select *Headers or Footers* options.

    Note: The Header and Footer Specifications options are displayed on the screen.

3. Press the number opposite the name of the header or footer that you need to edit.
4. Type 4 to edit the header.
5. Immediately press F7 to exit.
6. Press RETURN to return to the document.

    The margins in the header or footer will be adjusted automatically.

USING FOOTNOTES

WordPerfect automatically numbers footnotes. However, the new number option of the footnote menu can be used to change the footnote number.

A footnote can be up to 300 lines in length. However, it is recommended that footnotes be confined to a few lines so that they can easily be inserted on one page without interrupting the flow of text. WordPerfect will try to keep the entire footnote on the same page as its reference. However, if there is not enough room on the page for a footnote, the first three lines will be printed on the page and the remaining lines will appear on the next page. The options feature of the footnote menu can be used to adjust the line spacing of the footnote if desired.

The Block and Move commands may be executed while creating or editing a footnote.

Creating Footnotes

1. Position the cursor at the location where the reference to the footnote is to be inserted.
2. Hold down the CTRL key and press F7 to display the Footnote menu.

    The menu *1 Create; 2 Edit; 3 New #; 4 options; 5 Create Endnote; 6 Edit EndNote:* will appear at the bottom of the screen.

3. Type 1 to create the footnote.

    A blank screen will appear. The note number will be displayed in the upper left corner. Exit will be highlighted in the lower left corner.

4. Enter the text for the footnote.
5. Press F7 to leave the footnote and return to the main document.

Editing Footnotes

A footnote may be edited from anywhere in the document.

1. Hold down the CTRL key and press F7 to display the Footnote menu.

   The menu will appear at the bottom of the screen.

2. Type 2 to edit the footnote.

   The prompt *Ftn #* will appear at the lower left corner.

3. Press RETURN if the number is correct, otherwise enter the desired number or character and press RETURN.

   The footnote screen will appear.

4. Make the desired changes to the footnote text.

5. Press F7 to leave the footnote and return to the main document.

Changing the Footnote Number

A footnote may be edited from anywhere in the document.

1. Hold down the CTRL key and press F7 to display the Footnote menu.

   The menu will appear at the bottom of the screen.

2. Type 3 to change the footnote number.

   The prompt *Ftn #* will appear at the lower left corner.

3. Enter the new footnote number; press RETURN.

   If desired, asterisks (*) or pound (#) signs can be used instead of numbers.

Changing Footnote Margins

If the margins are changed in the main document, one of the two procedures below must be executed to adjust the margins in the footnote.

Changing All Footnote Margins in the Document

× This procedure is not available to educational users.

1. Hold down the CTRL key and press F2 to start the spelling checker.
2. Type 6 to begin the word count.

   When the count is completed, the margins are reset. The margins would also be reset if 3, Document, was selected.

35

Changing Selected Footnote Margins in the Document

To selectively change margins, edit each footnote whose margins are to be changed using the *Editing Footnotes* above. No text need be changed; the margins will be corrected when F7 is pressed to exit the text of the footnote.

Deleting a Footnote

1. Position the cursor on the note number.
2. Press the Del key.

   The prompt Delete [Note] will appear.
3. Press Y to delete the note or RETURN to keep it.

Entering and Editing Text

USING WORD WRAP

When entering text in WordPerfect, press the RETURN key only:

- To end a line that does not extend to the right margin.
- To end a paragraph.
- To insert a blank line.

When you enter text that extends beyond the right margin, WordPerfect automatically moves the extra words to the beginning of the next line. This is called **word wrap** because the text automatically continues or wraps to the next line.

WordPerfect knows exactly how long each line should be. When words are added to or deleted from a line, it will automatically reform the text when the cursor leaves the line so that each word is positioned properly within the paragraph.

Note: Do not press the RETURN key at the end of each line. When the RETURN key is pressed, it inserts a hard RETURN code. A hard RETURN always terminates a line. As a result, if you insert or delete text in a line that ends in a RETURN, WordPerfect cannot adjust the text automatically.

USING HYPHENATION

Hyphenation is used to divide words that are too long to fit at the end of the line. When right justification is on, it is sometimes necessary to hyphenate a word to create a pleasing line. When using a ragged right margin, hyphenation can be used to create relatively even lines.

Note: Hyphenation is turned off when you enter Version 4.1 of Word Perfect. It is turned on in the educational version.

Types of Hyphens

WordPerfect recognizes two types of hyphens.

- **Soft hyphens**, which print only when they are needed.
- **Hard hyphens**, which always print.

Since the position of a word may change when a line is edited, soft hyphens are usually used when entering text.

Turning Hyphenation On

Version 4.2 (and later) users may elect to have hyphens automatically inserted if desired.

1. Position the cursor at the location where you want to begin hyphenation.

   Note: To hyphenate the entire document, move the cursor to the first line in the document.

2. Hold down the SHIFT key and press F8.

   This prompt appears: *1 Tabs; 2 E-Tabs; 3 Margins; 4 Spacing; 5 Hyphenation; 6 Align Char*

3. Press 5 to select the Hyphenation menu.
4. Press 1 to turn hyphenation on.

   A beep will sound when WordPerfect encounters a word that needs to be hyphenated.

Version 4.2 (and Later) Users

On aided or *On auto* will be displayed near the beginning of the line. If *aided* is displayed, hyphenation is suggested, but not inserted unless the ESC key is pressed. (This was the only mode available to Version 4.1 users.) Auto mode automatically inserts hyphens where needed.

To change the mode:

5. Press 3 to selected aided or 4 to select auto mode.

Adjusting the Hyphenation Zone

The Hyphenation Zone

The **hyphenation zone** determines whether a word will be hyphenated or moved to the next line. If a word fits within the hyphenation zone, it is placed on the line. If the word overlaps outside of the zone, it is hyphenated so that part of the word is placed on the current line and the rest of the word is placed on the next line. For example, if the word "determine" extended beyond the hyphenation zone, it would be hyphenated so that "deter-" is placed on the current line and "mine" is placed on the next line. If hyphenation is turned off or if the word cannot be hyphenated, the word is moved to the next line.

The first hyphenation zone or **left zone** begins seven spaces before the right margin and ends at the right margin. So the 7th column from the right margin acts as a left hyphenation boundary.

The **right zone** defines the number of spaces that a word can extend beyond the right margin. It is originally set at 0. So the second hyphenation margin is the right margin.

If a word starts before or on the left hyphenation boundary (7) and crosses the right boundary, it is hyphenated. As it crosses the boundary, WordPerfect beeps, indicating that the word should be hyphenated. It then suggests a hyphenation. For example, if the word "determine" began on the left boundary, it would cross the right boundary. Since it could not fit on the current line without overlapping the right margin, it would be hyphenated.

If a word starts after the left boundary and extends beyond the right boundary, it is moved to the next line. For example, if "deter" began three columns from the end of the line, it would be moved to the next line.

Note: If you wish to let words extend a character or two beyond the right margin, you may do so by increasing the size of the right zone from 0 to another value, such as 1 or 2. For example, if the right zone were set at 0, words that overlapped the right margin would be moved to the next line or hyphenated. If the right zone were set at 2, "determine" would be placed on the current line, even though it extended two characters beyond the right margin.

When justification is off, a smaller zone should be used to create a more even right edge.

Defining the Hyphenation Zone

The original left zone is 7 spaces from the margin. The original right zone is zero (0). Different hyphenation zones may be used in different parts of the document.

1. Position the cursor at the location where the hyphenation zone is to take effect.
2. Hold down the SHIFT key and tap F8 once.
3. Press 5 to select the Hyphenation menu.
4. Press 3 to select the *Set H-Zone* option.
5. Enter the number of columns in the left zone.
6. Press RETURN.
7. Enter the number of columns that a word may extend beyond the right margin.
8. Press RETURN.

Inserting a Hyphen in a Word

If hyphenation is turned on, WordPerfect will beep and display a suggested a hyphenation when it encounters a word that is too long to fit on the line.

1. Use the right and left arrow keys to position the cursor at the location where the hyphen is to be inserted.

   Note: Do not move the cursor if you wish to use the hyphenation suggested by WordPerfect.

2. Press ESC to insert a soft hyphen in the document.
3. Press F1 to cancel the hyphen and move the word to the beginning of the next line. A blinking slash will be inserted in front of the word to indicate that hyphenation was canceled.

   Note: If you wish to insert a space instead of a hyphen, press HOME and then press the spacebar. The word will be separated at the cursor location.

Removing a Hyphen

Use this procedure to remove the cancel hyphen code (blinking slash). This code is inserted when you elect to wrap a word to the next line, rather than hyphenate it.

1. Position the cursor at the word to be hyphenated.
2. Hold down the ALT key and press F3.
3. Position the cursor on the character that follows the blinking slash (/).

   Note: You will not be permitted to delete a soft hyphen.

4. Press the backspace key (⟵).
5. Press RETURN to hide the codes again.

Turning Hyphenation Off

1. Position the cursor at the location where hyphenation is to end.
2. Hold down the the SHIFT key and press F8.
3. Press 5 to see the hyphenation options.
4. Press 2 to end hyphenation.

HYPHENATING PHRASES

When you need to hyphenate a phrase, such as father-in-law or souped-up, press the dash key once for each hyphen. WordPerfect will insert a hard hyphen to indicate that the hyphen must always be displayed.

ENTERING DASHES

A dash is twice as wide as a hyphen.

1. Hold down the HOME key and press the key that contains the hyphen sign once. This will insert a minus sign.
2. Release the home key and press the hyphen key again.

ENTERING A MINUS SIGN

Minus signs are used in arithmetic formulas.

1. Hold down the HOME key and press the key that contains the minus sign.

CENTERING TEXT ON THE PAGE

Use this procedure to center text vertically on the page.

1. Position the cursor at the top of the page.
2. Hold down the ALT key and press F3 to reveal the codes.
3. Verify that no codes precede the cursor. If necessary, adjust the cursor so that it precedes other codes on the page.
4. Press RETURN to hide the codes.
5. Hold down the ALT key and Press F8 to view the Page Format menu.
6. Press 3 to select the Center option.

7. Press RETURN to leave the Page Format menu.

CENTERING TEXT ON A LINE

Use this procedure to center new text between the right and left margin.

1. Position the cursor on the left margin if centering a line of text. If centering column headings, position the cursor at the visual center of the column.

   Caution: If the cursor is not at the left margin, the text will be centered between the cursor position and the right margin.

2. Hold down the SHIFT key and press F6 to begin centering.

   The cursor will move to the center of the line.

3. Type the text to be centered.

   Note: Skip this step if centering existing text.

4. Press RETURN to center new text or press the down arrow key (↓) to center existing text.

CENTERING BLOCKS OF TEXT

Use this procedure to center each line in a block of text.

1. Position the cursor at the beginning of the text that you need centered.
2. Hold down the ALT key and press F4 to enter block mode.
3. Use the cursor movement keys to move the cursor to the end of the block.
4. Hold down the SHIFT key and press F6 to begin centering.

   The prompt *[Center]? (Y/N): N* will appear.

5. Press Y to center each line in the block.

   Press RETURN to change your mind.

GOING TO A TAB AND ENTERING TEXT

1. Press the TAB key.

   The cursor will proceed to the next tab.

2. Enter the text that is to be aligned at the tab.

Going to a Tab and Aligning Numbers or Text with a Value

This procedure is most commonly used to align numbers on a decimal point. However, it can also be used to align text with a value. For example, to align the first name on the space between it and the last name.

1. Hold down the CTRL key and press F6.

    The cursor will proceed to the next tab, and the prompt *Align Char =* will appear on the prompt line.

2. Enter the text that is to appear to the left of the tab alignment character.

    The text will be pushed to the left as it is entered.

3. Enter the alignment character.

    Note: The column of text will be aligned on this character.

4. Enter the text, if any, that is to appear to the right of the tab alignment character in the column.

    The text will be pushed to the right.

INDENTING PARAGRAPHS

Use this procedure to indent the left margin of every line in a paragraph or to indent a single line. Indentation ends when a hard RETURN is encountered.

1. Position the cursor at the location where indentation is to begin.
2. Press F4.
3. Type the desired text. (Skip this step if you wish to indent existing text.)
4. Press RETURN to end the indent.

UNDOING INDENTATION FOR ONE OR MORE LINES OF TEXT

Use this procedure to indent the first line in a block of text differently than the rest of the block. If indentation is begun at the left margin, the first line of text appears even with the left margin and the remainder of the paragraph is indented under it. Indentation ends when a hard RETURN is encountered.

1. Position the cursor at the location where indentation is to begin.
2. Press F4 to begin the indent.
3. Hold down the SHIFT key and press the TAB key.

    Note: This will move the text left on tab stop.

4. Type the desired text.
5. Press RETURN to end the indent.

INDENTING THE LEFT AND RIGHT MARGINS OF A PARAGRAPH

Use this procedure to indent both the left and right margins of a block of text.

1. Position the cursor at the location where you wish the indent to begin.
2. Hold down the SHIFT key and press F4.
3. Type the desired text.
4. Press RETURN to end the indent.

INSERTING TEXT

WordPerfect will automatically insert text at the cursor location. If necessary, press the down arrow (↓) to cause the margins to be reformed.

TYPING OVER TEXT

1. Press INS to turn insertion off.

   Note: The word *Typeover* will appear in the left bottom corner of the screen.

2. Type the desired text.
3. Press INS again when you are ready to turn insertion on again.

INSERTING EXTRA BLANK LINES

1. Position the cursor at the location where the blank line is to be inserted.
2. Press RETURN.

DELETING A CHARACTER

1. Position the cursor on the character to be deleted.
2. Press the DEL key.

DELETING A WORD

1. Position the cursor on the word to be deleted.
2. Hold down the CTRL key and press the Backspace key.

DELETING TO THE END OF LINE

1. Position the cursor on the first character to be deleted.
2. Hold down the CTRL key and press the End key.

DELETING A BLANK LINE

1. Position the cursor at the beginning of the line to be deleted.
2. Press the DEL key.

   If the line is not deleted, it means that the line contains some spaces. Continue to press DEL until the line is deleted.

DELETING TO THE END OF PAGE

This command erases both text and codes.

1. Position the cursor on the first character that you wish to delete.
2. Hold down the CTRL key and press the PgDn key.

   The prompt *Delete Remainder of Page? (Y/N): N* will appear.

3. Press Y to delete the text or RETURN to change your mind.

DELETING A PAGE BREAK

1. Position the cursor at the beginning of the first line after the page break.
2. Press the backspace key (⟵).

DELETING A CODE

This procedure may be used to remove codes without revealing them. For example, it can be used to remove the underlining code without pressing ALT and F3 to display the code. If the procedure is used when codes are revealed on the screen, step 3 may be omitted, since no prompt will appear.

1. Position the cursor to the right of the code to be deleted.
2. Press the backspace key.
3. Type Y to respond to the prompt that appears.

COPYING OR MOVING A SENTENCE, PARAGRAPH, OR PAGE

Beginning with Version 4.2, this procedure may also be used to delete text.

1. Position the cursor on the sentence to be moved.
2. Hold down the CTRL key and press F4.
3. Press 1 to copy or move a sentence.
   Press 2 to copy or move a paragraph.
   Press 3 to copy or move the current page.
4. Press 1 to move the text; press 2 to copy it.

   Note: Version 4.2 users may delete text by pressing 3.

5. Move the cursor to the location where the sentence is to be inserted.
6. Hold down the CTRL key and press F4.
7. Press 5 to retrieve the text.

   The text will be inserted at the cursor location.

MANIPULATING BLOCKS OF TEXT (COPYING, MOVING, DELETING)

To manipulate a block of text, define the boundaries of the block by using the procedure below. Then enter the WordPerfect command or function that represents the activity to be performed. Command choices include:

- Bold
- Flush it right
- Print
- Spelling check
- Underline
- Center
- Replace
- Copy
- Mark it
- Save
- Sort
- Superscript
- Change case
- Delete
- Move
- Subscript
- Append

Note: Once the Block (ALT and F4) command has been used to identify a block of text, you may perform as many operations on it as desired. For example, the block can be copied into several locations in the text by repeating the copy procedure as many times as necessary.

Using Highlighting When Identifying Blocks of Text

The text in the block is highlighted to make it stand out from the rest of the document. Depending on the type of terminal used, **Highlighted** text is brighter, dimmer, or a different color than the surrounding text.

Defining a Block of Text

1. Position the cursor at the beginning of the block of text.
2. Hold down the ALT key and tap F4 once.

   Block on will blink in the bottom left corner of the screen.

3. Use the cursor movement keys to highlight all of the text to be included in the block.

   Note: Pressing the RETURN key will highlight to the nearest return. To highlight larger blocks of text, use the plus and minus keys and the PgUp and PgDn keys.

4. Enter the operation to be performed next.

   For example, press F4 to move or copy the block.

Canceling Highlighting

- If you accidentally highlight too many words in a line, tap the left arrow key until the extraneous words are no longer highlighted.
- If you accidentally highlight too many lines on the screen, tap the up arrow key until only the desired text is highlighted. To remove highlighting from a page or screen, tap the PgUp or minus (−) key.
- To turn all highlighting off or to cancel Block mode, press F1.

Displaying a Block of Text

To reuse/rehighlight a block of text that was marked earlier:

1. Hold down the ALT key and press F4 to turn Block on.
2. Hold down the CTRL key and press HOME twice.

   Go To is displayed, then the block is displayed.

Returning to the Beginning of a Block

1. Use the ALT and F4 keys to turn Block on if *Block on* is not flashing in the bottom left corner.
2. Hold down the CTRL key and press HOME.
3. Hold down the ALT key and press F4 to go to the beginning of the block.

   Press F1 if you have changed your mind.

DELETING A BLOCK OF TEXT

1. Use the ALT and F4 keys to identify the block as shown above.
2. Press DEL.
3. Type Y to delete the block of text.

   Press RETURN if you have changed your mind.

COPYING TEXT WITHIN A DOCUMENT

1. Use the ALT and F4 keys to identify the block as shown above.
2. Hold down the CTRL key and press F4 to select the Move function.
3. Type 2 to copy the block of text.
4. Move the cursor to the location where the text is to be inserted.
5. Hold down the CTRL key and press F4.
6. Type 5 to copy the text.
7. To copy the text more than once, repeat steps 4 through 6 as many times as needed.

COPYING TEXT FROM ONE DOCUMENT INTO ANOTHER

There are several ways to copy one document into another. You can retrieve a block of text that has been written to disk with the Save function, you can retrieve a document, or you can append a block of text onto the end of another document.

Inserting an Existing Document into Another

Use this procedure to copy a previously saved WordPerfect document into the document you are editing. If you wish to retrieve a non-WordPerfect document, use the Text In/Out function described in *Retrieving a Non-WordPerfect Document* in the *Document Filing and Housekeeping* chapter.

Note: If you do not know the document name, use the Retrieve option of the LIST function.

1. Position the cursor on the text to be inserted.
2. Hold down the SHIFT key and press F10.
3. Enter the name of the document to be retrieved.
4. Press RETURN.

   The document will be inserted at the cursor location.

Appending a Block of Text onto the End of Another Document

This procedure is used to define a block of text and then attach it to the end of another document.

1. Position the cursor at the beginning of the text to be inserted at the end of another document.
2. Hold down the ALT key and press F4.
3. Use the cursor movement keys to highlight all of the text to be copied.
4. Hold down the CTRL key and press F4.
5. Press 3 to select Append.
6. Enter the name of the document that the text is to be inserted into.
7. Press RETURN.

Moving or Copying a Column

This procedure applies to columns of text or numbers that were created by using the tab or indent keys. Do not use it to move newspaper columns created by using the COL DEF option of the Math/Columns function.

1. Hold down the ALT key and press F4.
2. Use the cursor keys to highlight the column of data that is to be moved.

   A column begins at one tab and is ended by another tab, a tab align, or a hard return.

3. Hold down the CTRL key and press F4 to select the Move function.
4. Press 4.
5. Press 1 to move the column.

   Press 2 to copy it.

Press 3 to delete it (Version 4.2 only).

6. Position the cursor at the location where the column is to be positioned.
7. Hold down the CTRL key and press F4.
8. Press 4 to retrieve the column.

Note: Columns to the right of this column are shifted one column to the next tab stop.

MOVING A BLOCK OF TEXT

WordPerfect uses a cut and retrieve process to move text. When the text is cut, it is removed from the document and stored in memory until it is retrieved.

1. Hold down the ALT key and press F4.
2. Use the cursor movement keys to highlight the block of text to be moved.
3. Hold down the CTRL key and press F4 to select the Move function.
4. Press 1 to *cut* the text from the document.

   Note: The text will disappear.

5. Position the cursor where the text is to be inserted.
6. Hold down the CTRL key and press F4.
7. Press 5 to *retrieve* the cut text.

   The text will be inserted at the cursor location.

CREATING NEWSPAPER AND PARALLEL COLUMNS

Newspaper columns are used to create text that flows from one column to another. Parallel columns are used for text that moves across columns, such as scripts or definitions. Column creation consists of two procedures: Defining the columns and Building the columns.

Defining Newspaper Columns

1. Hold down the ALT key and press F7 to select Text Columns.

   The Math/Columns menu will appear at the bottom of the screen.

2. Press 4 to select *Column Def*.
3. Type Y to create evenly spaced margins.

4. Enter the number of spaces to be left between columns.

Version 4.1 Users

5. Press RETURN to position the cursor after the question *Do you want groups left together on a page?*
6. Type N or press RETURN.

    Proceed to step 7.

Version 4.2 (or Later) Users

5. Position the cursor immediately after the column types.
6. Type 1 to indicate that a newspaper column format is to be used.
7. Enter the number of columns to appear on a page and press RETURN.

    WordPerfect will calculate and display the margins for each column.
8. To accept the settings, press RETURN once for each setting.

    After the last setting has been accepted, you will be returned to the Math/Column menu.
9. Skip the next procedure and proceed to the procedure *Building Columns*.

Defining Parallel Columns

1. Hold down the ALT key and press F7 to select Text Columns.

    The Math/Columns menu will appear at the bottom of the screen.
2. Press 4 to select *Column Def.*
3. Type N to create unevenly spaced margins.

Version 4.1 Users

4. Position the cursor after the question *Do you want groups left together on a page?*
5. Type Y.

    Proceed to step 6.

Version 4.2 (or Later) Users

5a. Position the cursor immediately after the column types.
5b. Enter 2 to indicate that parallel column format is to be used.

6. Type the number of columns to appear on a page and press RETURN.
7. Enter the left and right margin of each column opposite the appropriate column number. For example, opposite *Column 1*, type 10 to set a left margin of 10 and 20 to set a right margin of twenty—thus creating a column that is 10 positions in width.

   After the last setting has been entered, you will be returned to the Math/Column menu.
8. Proceed to the next procedure.

Building Columns

Block protection will be turned on to keep the contents of the columns together. To insert a page break where needed, hold down the CTRL key and press RETURN. The cursor will be positioned below the last row in the longest column.

> *Note*: This procedure assumes that you are in the Math/Columns menu and that you have executed one of the two previous procedures.

1. Press 3 to begin column mode.

   Col will appear on the status line, and a *[Col on]* indicator is placed in the text to identify the column being entered.
2. Type in the columns.
3. Hold down the ALT key and press F7 when you are done typing the columns in.
4. Type 3 to end column mode.

   [Col off] is inserted in the text and a hard page return is inserted for each empty column. The cursor will be placed at the left margin.

EDITING NEWSPAPER AND PARALLEL COLUMNS

The cursor movement keys will work normally inside each column except as noted below. The right and left boundaries of the column will be treated as if they were right and left boundaries on a page.

To Move between Columns

1. Hold down the CTRL key and press HOME.

   Go To will appear at the bottom of the screen.
2. Press the left arrow to move to the previous column.

Press the right arrow key to move to the next column.

Hold down Home and press the left arrow to proceed to the first column.

Hold down Home and press the right arrow to proceed to the rightmost column.

To Move within Columns

- To move from the bottom of the column to the top, press the right arrow key.
- To move from the top of the column to the bottom, press the left arrow key.

Moving and Copying Information within a Column

Use the Cut and Copy options on the Move (CTRL and F4) menu to move text within a column.

Moving and Copying Columns

Use the ALT and F4 keys to define the column as a block, and then use the Move command (CTRL and F4) to move or copy the text.

Warning: Do not use the cut and copy option of the Move menu to move or copy columns.

LOCATING INFORMATION/GLOBAL SEARCHES

F2 is used to search forward through the document for a **string** or group of characters. For example, the word *down* is a string of characters, 123 is a string of numbers.

To search backward through the document, hold down the SHIFT key and press F2.

Finding a Word or Pattern of Characters

This procedure can be used to locate a WordPerfect code or any combination of letters, numbers or special characters. For convenience, the group of characters searched for is called a **string** in the procedure below.

1. Press F2 to search forward from the cursor position through the document for the string.

   Hold down the SHIFT key and press F2 to search backward from the cursor position through the document for the string.

Srch appears in the lower left corner.

2. Enter the word or phrase that you wish to locate.

   If you are looking for a WordPerfect code, enter the desired code.

3. Press F2 to begin the search.

   The cursor will move to the end of the first occurrence of the string or code.

4. Take any desired action.

   To continue the search process, proceed to the next step. Otherwise, this ends the procedure.

5. Press F2 to display the forward search string.

   Hold down the ALT key and press F2 to search backward from the cursor position.

   Note: The string will be displayed.

6. If desired, enter a new search string.
7. Press F2 to begin the search.
8. Repeat steps 5 through 7 as often as desired.

   Not Found will be displayed at the left corner of the screen when all occurrences of the string have been located.

REPLACING INFORMATION

The Replace searches forward until it finds the desired string or group of characters. It then replaces it with the new string. *Note*: This function may also be used to delete a string.

Replacing Items in a Block

This procedure limits the search and replace area to a block of text. Text outside of the block will not be affected by the replace operation.

1. Hold down the ALT key and press F4 to select the Block function.
2. Use the cursor movement keys to mark the block.
3. Follow the search procedure below.

Replacing All or Just Some Items

1. Hold down the ALT key and press F2 to invoke Replace.

   The prompt *W/Confirm? (Y/N): N* will appear.

2. Press Y to selectively replace items. This response causes WordPerfect to display each occurrence of the item and then ask for confirmation that the item is to be replaced.

   Press RETURN to replace every occurrence of the item automatically.

   The *Srch* prompt will appear.

3. Enter the word, phrase, or code that you wish to replace.

   Note: Do not enter anything if you wish to use the string that is displayed.

4. Press F2.

   The prompt *Replace With* will appear.

5. Enter the word, phrase, or code that is to replace the original text.

   Note: Do not enter anything if you wish to delete the original code.

6. Press F2.

   If *Confirm = Y* was entered when you began the replace process, the first occurrence of the item is displayed and the prompt *Confirm? (Y/N): N* appears. Enter Y to replace the item.

Deleting Every Occurrence of An Item

Follow the above procedure, but do not enter a replacement phrase when prompted in step 5. Instead, press F2.

ADJUSTING THE AMOUNT OF TEXT ON A PAGE/PAGINATION

WordPerfect automatically inserts page breaks when the page is full. The following procedures permit you to manually adjust the pagination process.

Forcing a Page Break

WordPerfect will automatically advance to a new page when the specified limit of lines is reached. If you need to end a page sooner, use this procedure.

1. Position the cursor at the position where the page break is to occur.

2. Hold down the CTRL key and press RETURN.

Keeping Text Together/Conditional Page Break

Use this procedure to keep headings with text or to keep items in a list together on a page.

1. Position the cursor on the line above the beginning of the group of text that is to be kept together.
2. Hold down the ALT key and press F8 to select the Page Format menu.
3. Press 9 to select Conditional End of Page.

    The prompt *Number of lines to keep together =* will appear.

4. Enter the number of lines that are to be kept together on the same page.

    Caution: If blank lines separate the text, be sure to include the blank lines in the count.

5. Press RETURN twice.

Preventing a Page Break within a Block of Text

Use this procedure to keep a block of text together.

Caution: Do not use this option casually, since if it is used too often, you will in effect become responsible for manually creating the proper page breaks on all pages.

1. Position the cursor at the beginning of the group of text that is to be kept together.
2. Hold down the ALT key and press F4 to select the Block command.
3. Use the cursor movement keys to move to the end of the block of text that is to be kept together.
4. Hold down the ALT key and press F8 to select Page Format.
5. Press Y.

Creating Special Text Effects

Special text effects are used to emphasize text by making it appear darker, underlining it, or changing its position on the page. They can also be used to create new characters by typing two characters in the same position.

CREATING BOLD TEXT

Bold text is darker than normal text. The printer produces this effect by striking the character twice. Once the bold code is entered, text is printed in boldface until another bold code is encountered.

Entering Bold Text

Use this procedure when entering new text.

1. Position the cursor at the location where bold text is to begin.
2. Press F6 to insert a begin bold code into the text.
3. Enter the text that is to be placed in boldface.

   Note: The text will be highlighted as you type it. Depending on the type of terminal used, it will be brighter, dimmer, or a different color than the surrounding text.

4. Press F6 to end bold.

Changing Existing Text to Bold Text

Use this procedure to change text to bold text. (× This procedure does not work with the educational version.) Run a test to see whether it works for your version before using it.

1. Position the cursor at the beginning of the text that is to be placed in boldface.
2. Press F6 to insert a begin bold code into the text.

   Note: The text will not be highlighted on the screen.

3. Position the cursor at the end of the text that is to be placed in bold face.
4. Press F6 to end bold.

USING SUBSCRIPTS AND SUPERSCRIPTS

Subscripts print slightly below the other text on the line while **superscripts** print slightly above it.

Note: When Subscript or Superscript is selected from the Super/Subscript menu, only the next character is raised or lowered. To raise or lower a word, phrase, or other block of characters, use the appropriate Advance option. Unlike Subscript and Superscript, once Advance is turned on, it is in effect until it is turned off.

Warning: These options are not supported on all printers. Before using any option extensively, create one example and see if it prints properly on your printer.

1. Position the cursor at the location where the text is to be adjusted.
2. Hold down the SHIFT key and press F1 to display the Super/subscript menu.
3. Press 1 (Superscript) to raise one character.

   Press 2 (Subscript) to lower one character.

   Press 3 to overstrike one character with another.

   Press 4 (advance upward) to raise text one-half line.

   Note: △ will appear in the lower left corner.

   Press 5 (advance downward) to lower text one-half line.

   Note: ▽ will appear in the lower left corner.

   Press 6 to advance the text more than one half line; press 6 and then enter the number of the line which is to be skipped to.

4. Enter the text to be printed.

   The text will not appear any differently on the screen, but if codes are revealed, the appropriate code appears in front of the text.

5. Press 4 (Advance Upward) if option 5 was selected earlier to print text below the current line. (This returns the text to normal by raising it one half line.)

   Press 5 (Advance Downward) if you were printing text above the current line and now wish to return it to the line.

UNDERLINING TEXT

The Underline command can be used to either automatically underline text as you type or to underline an existing block of text.

You can change the appearance of your underlining by selecting one of four styles.

- **Non-continuous** underlining underlines characters and spaces, but does not underline tabs. This is the most common form of underlining.
- **Continuous** underlining underlines characters, spaces, and tabs. This type of underlining is most commonly used to create solid lines on a report or chart.
- **Single** underlining types one line under the character being underlined.
- **Double** underlining types two lines under a character.

Note: This type of underlining is not supported on all printers. If it is used, a single underline will appear on the screen when the text is typed, but a double underline will be printed.

Selecting an Underlining Style

See the preceding paragraphs for a description of the underlining style options.

1. Hold down the CTRL key and press F8 to display the Print Format menu.
2. Press 5 to select *Non-continuous single* if you wish to underline characters and spaces with a single underline.

   Press 6 to select *Non-continuous double* if you wish to underline characters and spaces with a double underline.

   Caution: Be sure that this feature is supported by your printer.

Press 7 to select *Continuous single* if you wish to underline tabs, spaces, and characters with a single underline.

Press 8 to select *Continuous double* if you wish to underline tabs, spaces, and characters with a double underline.

Caution: Be sure that this feature is supported by your printer.

3. Press RETURN when you are ready to return to your document.

Underlining Text as You Type

This procedure causes text to be underlined as it is entered.

1. Press F8 to begin underlining.

   Note: The number after Pos will be underlined on the status line.

   Note: The [U][u] codes are used to identify the start and end points. The [*Undrl Style:*] code indicates the style of underlining used. Different styles may be used within a document. These codes appear when the Reveal Codes (ALT and F3) command is used. The style code is activated when the text is printed.

2. Enter the text to be underlined.

   The text will be underlined on the screen. However, the underlining style used on the screen may differ from the style that will be used when the document is printed. To verify the style, use the ALT and F3 keys to examine the style code.

Stopping Automatic Text Underlining

1. Hold down F8 when you wish to stop automatically underlining the text.

   The underline codes will be placed at the end of the text to mark the end of the underlined area.

Underlining Existing Text

This procedure underlines existing text.

1. Position the cursor at the beginning of the text to be underlined.
2. Hold down the ALT key and press F4 to select the Block command.
3. Use the cursor movement keys to highlight the text to be underlined.
4. Press F8 to underline the text.

   The text will be underlined on the screen.

Note: The [U][u][*Undrl Style:*] codes will appear at the beginning and ending of the block when the Reveal Codes command is used. When printed, the text will be underlined in the style that you selected.

REMOVING UNWANTED UNDERLINING

There are two ways to remove underlining. Both are shown below.

Revealing the Code and Then Removing It

1. Position the cursor at the location where underlining is to end.
2. Hold down Alt and press F3 to reveal the codes.
3. Use the cursor movement keys to move the cursor next to the underline code ([U][u]).
4. Press DEL if the cursor is to the left of the code. Otherwise, press the Backspace key to delete the code.

   As soon as you delete one of the U's ([U] or [u]), the other will disappear.

5. Press RETURN to return to normal document screen.

Removing Underlining without Revealing Codes

This technique can be used to delete any code.

1. Position the cursor at the beginning of the underlined text.
2. Look at the Status line and verify that the Pos number is underlined. If not, press the right arrow (→) and see whether an underline appears under the Pos number. If it is still not underlined, experiment with pressing the left and right arrows until the Pos number is underlined.
3. Press the Backspace key.

   Note: The prompt *Delete [Undrline]? (Y/N): N* will appear.

4. Press Y to delete the underlining or RETURN to change your mind.

Printing

PRINTING A DOCUMENT

WordPerfect provides several different methods of printing, including printing the current entire document or only the page on which the cursor is located; printing the entire document or specified pages of the document from disk; and printing a marked block of text. Envelopes and forms that are normally suited to word processing can be typed by using the Type-Thru feature. All printing should be completed before exiting from WordPerfect.

Printing the Current Document

It is possible to work on a document while it is printing.

1. Hold down the SHIFT key and press F7.

    The following menu appears at the bottom of the screen:

    1 Full Text; 2 Page; 3 Change Options; 4 Printer Control; 5 Type-thru: 0

2. Type 1 to print the entire document.

    A copy of the entire document file is created in memory or, if the computer memory does not have enough room, on the default disk. If the disk does not have enough room for a copy of the complete document, a *disk full* error message appears on screen.

3. Type 2 to print the current page.

The entire page is printed, not just the part displayed on screen.

The document will be printed as soon as the printer is available.

Printing a Portion of a Document

A portion of text can be printed by marking the specified block of text and then printing it.

1. Position the cursor at the beginning to the block of text to be printed.
2. Hold down the ALT key and press the F4 key (Block key).

    A flashing *Block on* message appears on screen in the lower left corner.

3. Position the cursor at the end of the block of text to be printed.

    The text to be printed is highlighted on screen.

4. Hold down the SHIFT key and press the F7 key.

    The Status Line is displayed on screen and a prompt asking if the block is to be printed.

5. Type Y.

    A ** Please Wait ** message appears on screen.

6. Press the F1 key to cancel the Block mode once the printer starts.
7. Resume editing while the block of text is being printed.

    It is possible to continue working on a document while a job is being printed.

Printing a Document Stored on Disk

A document printed from disk is printed as it was last saved. Any changes made in the current file displayed on screen are NOT printed unless the document is first saved to disk and then printed. Printing from an existing disk file does NOT require additional memory, as no temporary file is created.

A document may also be printed from disk by selecting the Print option of the F5 (LIST) function. However, if this option is chosen, the print menu does not appear, and no defaults can be changed.

1. Hold down the SHIFT key and press the F7 key.

    The printer menu selections appear at the bottom of the screen display.

2. Type 4 to display the Printer Control menu.

   The Printer Control menu is displayed on screen.

3. If you need to change printers, type 1 to select print options. Then type 1 and enter the number of the printer to be used.

4. Enter P to print the document.

   The cursor is positioned under the *Selection* prompt, and the prompt *Document name* appears.

5. Enter the name of the document to be printed. Press RETURN.

   If the file is stored on a drive other than the default drive, the disk drive letter and a colon should precede the name of the file.

   Example: B:Filename

   The prompt *Starting Page*: will appear.

   × *Note*: The Educational disk version displays the prompt *all*. Press RETURN once to print the document.

6. Enter the starting page number and press RETURN, or press RETURN to accept the number displayed.

   The prompt *Ending Page:* will appear.

7. Enter the number of the last page to be printed and press RETURN.

   Note: Press RETURN without entering anything to print to the end of the document.

8. Press RETURN to leave this menu.

Printing More Than One Document

The documents will be printed in the order in which they are selected for printing. Additional documents may be selected while the first document is being printed. The *Job List* section of the Printer Control Screen displays the name of each document to be printed and its corresponding job number.

1. Execute the preceding procedure to select the first document to be printed.
2. Repeat steps 3 through 8 to select additional documents to be printed.
3. Press RETURN to leave this menu.

Printing Multiple Copies of a Document

The Change Options menu can also be accessed from the Printer Control menu by typing a 1 to select the Print Options menu.

1. Hold down the SHIFT key and press the F7 key.

   The print menu appears at the bottom of the screen.

2. Type 3 to change print options.
3. Type 2 to select the copies option.
4. Enter the number of copies to be printed. Press the RETURN key.

   Caution: Every print job will be printed with the specified number of copies until you exit WordPerfect or change the number of copies again.

5. Press RETURN to leave this menu.

Stopping a Print Job

1. Press S to interrupt the printing process.

   The printer is stopped and remains so until you enter G to resume printing.

Resume Printing a Job That Has Been Stopped Previously

The Job Status Line reads *Waiting for a "Go"* to indicate that the printer is waiting for the command to resume printing.

1. Advance the paper to the beginning of a new page.
2. Type G to have the printer resume printing.

   The document is printed from the beginning.

Canceling a Print Job

1. Press C.

   The Selection prompt displays the following message:

   Cancel which job? (* = All jobs)

2. Enter the job number to cancel a specific job or an * (asterisk) to cancel all waiting jobs. Press RETURN.

   If an asterisk is entered, the following prompt appears:

   Cancel all print jobs? (Y/N): N

3. Type Y to cancel all jobs.

Printing a Job out of Sequence
(Rush Print Job Option)

It is possible to print a job out of sequence with the **Rush Print Job** option. It is not necessary to cancel the print jobs that precede the needed print job on the list.

1. Type R when the Printer Control menu is displayed on screen, even if a document is currently being printed.

   A prompt appears asking which job to rush.

2. Enter the job number of the document to be rushed. Press RETURN.

   A second prompt asks whether the current job should be interrupted.

3. Press Y to stop printing the current document.

   Printing of the current document is stopped and printing of the needed rush document begins. Printing of the current job is resumed, starting at the top of the page it was printing when stopped.

   or

3. Press N to continue printing the current job and then print the needed rush job.

Displaying All Print Jobs Waiting

The Job List displayed on the Printer Control Menu displays only three print jobs. The bottom line of the menu reads:

Additional Jobs not shown: 0

If a number other that 0 is displayed on this line, other jobs are on the list to be printed.

1. Type D to display the complete Job List of documents to be printed.

TYPEWRITER MODE

Text that has been typed with the Type-thru feature is NOT retained in memory nor stored in a disk file.

Some of the printers supported by WordPerfect cannot use the Type-thru feature (such as the Cannon Laser and the Hewlett Packard Laser Jet printers). Other printers are limited to using the line by line option only (such as the Brother HR1, the Epson LQ-1500, the Epson RX-80, Texas Instruments 855, the Okidata Microline 84, and the MPI Printmate).

Line by Line Type-thru

Line by line Type-thru has an advantage over character by character Type-thru: typing mistakes may be corrected on screen before the RETURN key is pressed and the line is sent to the printer.

1. Hold down the SHIFT key and press the F7 key.

    The print menu options appear at the bottom of the screen.

2. Enter 5 to select Type-thru.

    A prompt asks you to select *by line or by character* printing.

3. Enter 1 to select the line by line option.

    The Line Type-thru Printing menu appears on screen.

4. Position the form, paper, or envelope in the printer so that the printhead is placed on the first line to be printed.
5. Position the cursor by pressing the spacebar until the cursor indicates where the text is to begin.
6. Type the first line of text and verify that there are no typing mistakes.
7. Press the RETURN key.

    The line of text is printed, and the printhead is advanced to the next line.

8. Repeat steps 6 and 7 until all text has been entered.
9. Press the F7 key when you are finished typing.

Correcting Typing Mistakes before Printing

Cursor movements using the Type-thru feature are more limited than those used in the Edit mode.

- Left arrow: moves the cursor one character to the left.
- Right arrow: moves the cursor one character to the right.
- Press Home and left arrow: moves cursor to beginning of line.
- Press Home and right arrow: moves cursor to end of line.
- Up or down arrow: moves the printhead up or down a line on your paper on some printers. The Up Arrow feature does not work on all printers.
- Press the RETURN key to move the paper down by a line.

Clearing Characters from the Screen

1. Hold down the CTRL key and press the PgDn key.

TEMPORARILY INSTALLING A PRINTER

× This feature is disabled on the educational version.

1. Hold down the SHIFT key and press F7.

   The print menu appears at the bottom of the screen display.

2. Type 4.

   The Printer Control menu is displayed on screen.

3. Type 3 to select a printer.

   The cursor is positioned after the line:

   Printer 1, Using Definition 1.

4. If the printer that you wish to use is defined, enter the number opposite the specific printer model that you are using. Otherwise, press PgDn to view the list of supported printers, and type the number that is displayed to the left of your printer.

   The number appears after the words *Using Definition:* on the Select Printers menu and the printer definition is copied from the Printer diskette onto your default diskette.

   Note: If a message appears that says that the program cannot find the printer files, place the WordPerfect Printer diskette in the disk drive and type the appropriate disk drive letter. A list of printers will be displayed on screen.

5. Type 1 to select a parallel port (LPT1).

   If you are using a serial or a laser printer or more than one printer that requires a parallel port, select the appropriate option displayed.

6. Type 1 to select Continuous feed.

   If a printer is hand fed or sheet fed, select the appropriate option.

   The Printer Definition Screen and the name of the printer definition just installed appears at the top of the screen.

7. Press the F7 key to exit the Printer Control Screen. The document in use prior to the printer installation is displayed on screen.

Changing Printers

× This feature is disabled on the educational version.

1. Hold down the SHIFT key and press the F7 key.

The print menu appears at the bottom of the screen display.

2. Type 3 to change options temporarily.

   The Change Print Options Temporarily menu appears on the screen.

3. Type 1 and enter the number of the printer to be used to change printers.
4. Press the RETURN key.

   The selected printer is used to print the current document only. The default printer is used for all print jobs after the current one.

USING MACROS TO LINK AND PRINT SEVERAL DOCUMENTS

This procedure allows you to link several documents together before printing. It is particularly useful with the educational version of WordPerfect where the size of saved documents is limited. By using this procedure with the educational version, documents of any length can be printed.

1. Use the F7 key to clear the screen.
2. Hold down the CTRL key and press F10.

   Define Macro: appears at the bottom left-hand corner of the screen.

3. Enter a name for the macro, for example, PRINTJOB, and press RETURN.
4. Hold down the SHIFT key and press F10.
5. Enter the name of the first document to be printed.
6. Continue pressing the PgDn key until the cursor is at the end of the document.
7. Repeat steps 4 through 6 for each document to be combined.

   Note: List the documents in the order that they are to be printed.

8. Hold down the CTRL key and press F10 to complete the definition of the macro.
9. To print the documents, enter SHIFT F7 and select option 1 from the menu.
10. To retrieve a macro, hold down the ALT key and press F10.

    Macro: appears at the bottom left-hand corner of the screen.

11. Enter your name for the macro, for example PRINTJOB, and press RETURN.

The Spelling Checker and the Thesaurus

USING THE SPELLING CHECKER

The Spelling Checker of WordPerfect contains three dictionaries: a common word list, which contains approximately 1550 words; a main word list; and a supplemental word list. The dictionary contains more than 100,000 words in the three lists.

× The spelling checker provided with the educational version has a very limited dictionary.

Words that are not contained in any of the three lists can be added to the supplemental word list for future reference. Many proper names are in the dictionary, but names of cities are not included.

WordPerfect always searches the common word list first, then the main list, and finally the supplemental list. Words not found in the dictionary are indicated by a message displayed on the Status Line with suggested possible replacements.

The Spelling Checker can be used to verify spelling in an entire document, a page, a block, or a single word. It is possible to look up a word before it is entered in the document, to look up a word using the phonetic option, or to display the total word count.

CHECKING THE SPELLING IN A DOCUMENT

The total word count is displayed when the Speller is finished.

1. Hold down the SHIFT key and press F10 to retrieve the document file to be checked.
2. Insert the Speller diskette into the B: drive.
3. Hold down the CTRL key and press F2.

   The following menu is displayed on screen on the Status Line:

   Check: 1 Word; 2 Page; 3 Document; 4 Change Dictionary; 5 Look Up; 6 Count

4. Type 1 to check the spelling of the word at the cursor location. Type 2 to check the spelling of the displayed page. Type 3 to check the entire document.

   The message * *Please Wait* * appears on the Status Line.

   Misspelled words or words not contained in the dictionary are highlighted in reverse video on the screen, as they are encountered. The following prompt appears on the bottom of the screen:

   Not Found! Select Word or Menu Option (0=Continue): 0
   1 Skip Once; 2 Skip; 3 Add Word; 4 Edit; 5 Look Up; 6 Phonetic

   A list of suggested replacements beneath a double line of dashes is also displayed on screen.

5. If the desired word is displayed in the list of replacements, type the letter next to the correct replacement.

   If the word is NOT contained in the list of suggested replacements do one of the following:

   - Type 1 to accept this single occurrence of the word.

   The Spelling Checker will stop each time it finds this word in the document.

   - Type 2 to accept the word wherever it is found in the document.
   - Type 3 to add the word to the Supplemental List.
   - Type 4 to revise the text. (Press RETURN to resume the spelling check.)

   The Spelling Checker will verify the revised text and allow you to select another option from the menu if the revised text is incorrect.

- Type 5 to look up a word pattern when you are not sure of the exact spelling.

Note: When entering the word pattern, use an * to replace the part of the word you do not know how to spell. Example: cons*e will display all words that begin with "con" and end with "e."

- Type 6 to display a list of words that sounds like the misspelled word.

Correcting Double Word Occurrences

The Spelling Checker highlights both words when a double word usage occurs. To correct the error, take one of the actions below.

1. Type 3 to select Option 3 of the Spelling Checker Menu and delete the second occurrence of the word.
2. If the double word is correct, do one of the following:
   - select option 1 to skip only this occurrence of the word or
   - select option 2 to skip the word throughout the document.

THE THESAURUS

The Thesaurus is used to clarify the exact meaning of a word. A list of synonyms appears on screen when a word is found in the Thesaurus. The list of synonyms is classified into groups of nouns, adjectives, and verbs and subdivided into groups of the same connotation. The Thesaurus contains more than 10,000 *headwords* (words that can be found in the Thesaurus).
x This list is very limited in the educational version.
The Thesaurus can be used to look up words in the text, words that are entered from the keyboard, or words that are displayed on the list of synonyms.

Looking Up a Word Contained in a Document

1. Position the cursor on the word to be looked up.

   If the cursor is not on a word, the Thesaurus will prompt you for a word when the menu is displayed.

2. Insert the Thesaurus disk in drive B.
3. Hold down the ALT key and press the function key F1.
4. Proceed to the next procedure.

Using the Thesaurus

Four lines of document text are displayed at the top of the screen. The bottom of the screen contains a list of synonyms for the word that you are looking up. The synonyms are grouped by part of speech: nouns (n), verbs (v), and adjectives and adverbs (a). Each group is separated by a solid line. The word being looked up will be highlighted at the top of each group. Not all parts of speech may be displayed for any given word. Highlighted letters precede entries in the first column.

The word being looked up is highlighted in the text and, if found in the Thesaurus, is called a **headword**. If it is not found in the Thesaurus, the error message *Not a headword* appears.

On the displayed list of words, words preceded by dots are also headwords. These words also have a list of synonyms that are contained in the Thesaurus.

Selecting a Word: Moving through the Thesaurus

5. Examine the lists of synonyms for a suitable word.
6. Use the up arrow, down arrow, left arrow, right arrow, PgUp, PgDn, +, and − keys to move through the columns.

Selecting a Word: Looking Up Variations

If the list does not contain the needed word, the list of possible choices can be expanded by looking up variations of the displayed synonyms or headwords.

7. Use the right or left arrow keys to position the cursor in the same column as the word to be looked up.

    Note: The highlighted letters will follow the cursor.

8. Type the letter next to the word to be looked up to display the list of synonyms for that word.

    The word must be a headword, that is, preceded by a dot. Otherwise, the error message *Not a Headword* is displayed.

    A new list of synonyms will replace whatever is currently displayed on screen in the second column. The next time a word is looked up, a new list will replace whatever is in the third column. To erase the information in the columns, press 4.

    Note: If desired, you can search for synonyms of headwords in the new list.

9. Repeat steps 6 and 7 as often as desired.

    If a suitable word is located, proceed to *Replacing the Word in the Document with a Selected Word*.

If a suitable word is not located, either enter another word using the procedure *Looking Up a Word Not Contained on a Displayed List* or look for another synonym by using the procedure *Looking through the Document for Other Words*.

10. Press RETURN or F7 to return to the document.

Moving a Displayed Column of Synonyms Up or Down

1. Press the PgUp, PgDn, Screen Up, or Screen Down key to move a column up or down.

Replacing the Word in the Document with a Selected Word

When the ALT key and F1 are entered to display the Thesaurus lists of synonyms, the bottom line of the screen contains the prompt:

1 Replace Word; 2 View Doc; 3 Look Up Word; 4 Clear Column: 0

1. Type 1 to replace the word at the current cursor location with one of the words on the displayed Thesaurus list.
2. Type the letter displayed to the left of the selected word.

   If there is no letter next to the word, move the cursor to the column containing the word. The letters will follow the cursor.
3. Exit from the Thesaurus screen without replacing a word by pressing the function key F7 or F1 or by pressing the spacebar or the RETURN key.

Looking through the Document for Other Words

When the ALT key and F1 are entered to display the Thesaurus lists of synonyms, the bottom line of the screen contains the prompt:

1 Replace Word; 2 View Doc; 3 Look Up Word; 4 Clear Column: 0

1. Type 2 to temporarily leave the Thesaurus and position the cursor on the next word of the document to be located.
2. Hold down the ALT key and press the function key F1 to look up the word at which the cursor is positioned,

   or

2. Press the function key F7, F1, or the RETURN key to return to the Thesaurus screen without looking up another word.

Looking Up a Word Not Contained on a Displayed List

When the ALT key and F1 are entered to display the Thesaurus lists of synonyms, the bottom line of the screen contains the prompt:

1 Replace Word; 2 View Doc; 3 Look Up Word; 4 Clear Column: 0

1. Type 3 to look up a word.

   The prompt *word:* is displayed.

2. Enter the word to be looked up. Press RETURN.

   Press RETURN or F1 if you decide not to enter a word.

   A list of synonyms will be displayed in a column to the right of the first group in the previous lookup. If the columns are not cleared between searches, the columns fills from left to right. When the third column is full, it is overwritten.

3. If the list is no longer needed, press 4 to clear the columns.
4. Exit the Thesaurus by pressing the function key F7 or F1.

Erasing the Columns

Columns are not always refreshed with each look-up. If the information in a column is not needed, use this procedure to clear the columns before looking up another word.

1. Type 4 to erase the references displayed in the columns on the screen.

   The screen is cleared.

Working with Multiple Documents

USING WINDOWS AND SCREENS

WordPerfect permits you to work on two documents at the same time. You may choose either to switch back and forth between documents or to split the screen into two parts or **windows** and view both documents at the same time. You may also use the split screen to examine different parts of the same document.

SWITCHING BETWEEN TWO DOCUMENTS

Switching documents is useful when you need to build two documents at the same time or to copy several parts of one document into another.

The document number that is displayed at the bottom right of the screen indicates which document is currently in use. When WordPerfect is entered, *Doc 1* is displayed at the bottom of the screen to indicate that the first document is in use.

1. To edit an existing document, hold down the SHIFT key and press F10 to retrieve the first document. Otherwise, enter the desired text and proceed to step 3.

    The *Document to be Retrieved* prompt will appear.

2. Enter the name of the document to be edited. Press RETURN.

   There will be a slight delay while the document is retrieved.

3. Hold down the SHIFT key and press F3 to invoke the SWITCH document command.

   A blank screen will appear. Doc 2 will be displayed at the bottom of the screen.

4. Hold down the SHIFT key and press F10 to retrieve a second document. Otherwise, enter the desired text and proceed to step 6.

   The *Document to be Retrieved* prompt will appear.

5. Enter the name of the second document that you wish to work with. Press RETURN.

   There will be a slight delay while the document is retrieved.

6. To return to the first document, hold down the SHIFT key and press F3 to invoke the SWITCH command.

TRANSFERRING TEXT BETWEEN TWO DOCUMENTS

This procedure shows how use the Switch function to copy text from one document into another document. It could also be used to move text from one document to another. Most WordPerfect Move or Copy commands could be used in a similar fashion to transfer text between two documents.

Text can also be moved between two documents by using the Append option of the Block menu or by writing it to disk and then retrieving it.

1. Position the cursor at the beginning of the text to be copied.
2. Hold down the ALT key and press F4 to invoke the Block command.
3. Use the cursor keys to highlight the text to be copied.
4. Hold down the CTRL key and press F4 to invoke the Move menu.
5. Press 2 to copy the information.
6. Hold down the SHIFT key and press F3 to invoke the SWITCH command.

   The second document will appear. Doc 2 will be displayed at the bottom of the screen.

7. Position the cursor at the location where the text to be inserted.
8. Hold down the CTRL key and press F4 to invoke the Move menu.
9. Press 5 to retrieve the text that you marked in step 3.
10. When you wish to return to the other document, hold down the SHIFT

key and press F3 to invoke the SWITCH command.

SPLITTING THE SCREEN/WINDOWS

The screen can be divided into two sections or **windows**. You can then work with a different document, or a view a different part of the same document, in each window.

Opening a Window

Use this procedure to divide the screen into two windows and then display a different document in each window. To view the same document in both windows, see the next procedure.

1. Hold down the CTRL key and press F3 to invoke the Screen command.

   The menu below will appear at the bottom of the screen.

   0 Rewrite; 1 Window; 2 Line draw; 3 Ctrl/Alt keys; 4 Colors; 5 Auto Rewrite: 0

2. Press 1 to select the *Window* option.

   The prompt *# Lines in this Window: 24* will appear.

3. Type the number of lines that you wish the top window to contain.

   Note: The default is 24, the number of lines on a screen. To divide the screen into two equal parts, enter 12.

4. Press RETURN.

   The screen will be divided into two windows, separated by a ruler line. Document 1 will appear in the top window. Document 2 will appear in the bottom window. The cursor will be positioned in the top window.

   The cursor movement keys and command keys work the same as they do when only one window is displayed.

Viewing the Same Document in Two Windows

To display the same document in two windows, the same document is placed in document 1 and document 2. Then the windows option is used to display document 1 and document 2 on the same screen.

1. If the screen is clear and you wish to edit an existing document, hold down the SHIFT key and press F10 to retrieve the first document. Otherwise, enter any desired text and proceed to step 3.

Warning: If you have begun working with the document, save the document (F10) before proceeding. This ensures that the same version of the document will appear in both screens.

The *Document to be Retrieved* prompt will appear.

2. Enter the name of the document to be edited. Press RETURN.

   There will be a slight delay while the document is retrieved.

3. Hold down the SHIFT key and press F3 to invoke the SWITCH command.

   A blank screen should appear. Doc 2 will be displayed at the bottom. If a document appears, press F7 and follow the Exit prompts to clear the screen.

4. Hold down the SHIFT key and press F10 to select the Retrieve function.

   The *Document to be Retrieved* prompt will appear.

5. Enter the name of the same document that you are working with in the Doc 1 work space. Press RETURN.

   There will be a slight delay while the document is retrieved.

6. Use the cursor movement keys to move through the document until the desired text is displayed.

   Warning: Do not edit document 2 or save it!

   The purpose of this document is to provide a different view of the same document as is stored in Doc 1. You can display different parts of the document, but you must not attempt to modify it.

7. Hold down the SHIFT key and press F3 to return to Doc 1.
8. Hold down the CTRL key and press F3 to invoke the screen command.

   The menu below will appear at the bottom of the screen.

   0 Rewrite; 1 Window; 2 Line draw; 3 Ctrl/Alt keys; 4 Colors; 5 Auto Rewrite: 0

9. Press 1 to select the *Window* option.

   The prompt *# Lines in this Window: 24* will appear.

10. Type the number of lines allocated to the top window.

    Note: To divide the screen into 2 equal parts, enter 12.

11. Press RETURN.

    The screen will be divided into two windows, separated by a ruler line. Document 1 will appear in the top window. Document 2 will appear in the bottom window. The cursor will be positioned in the top window (Doc 1). **Do not modify any text in the second document (Doc 2) during this procedure.**

The cursor movement keys and command keys work the same as they do when one window is displayed.

12. When you are done editing the first document:

    a) Verify that Doc 1 is displayed at the bottom of the active window.

    b) Use the Save function (F10) to save the document. **Do not save the contents of Doc 2.**

Moving between Windows

The ruler line will reflect the settings of the current window.

1. Hold down SHIFT and press F3 to invoke the switch command.

   The cursor will jump to the other window.

   The cursor movement keys and command keys will work the same as they did when only one window was displayed.

2. Hold down SHIFT and press F3 to return to other window.

Closing a Window

The current document will be displayed on the screen at the end of this procedure. The bottom window will be closed. To view the other document, hold down the SHIFT key and press F3 to Switch between documents.

1. Hold down the CTRL key and press F3 to invoke the screen command.

   The menu below will appear at the bottom of the screen.

   0 Rewrite; 1 Window; 2 Line draw; 3 Ctrl/Alt keys; 4 Colors; 5 Auto Rewrite: 0

2. Press 1 to select the *Window* option.

   The prompt *# Lines in this Window:* will appear.

3. Type 24 to restore the full screen.
4. Press RETURN.

81

Creating Form Documents

FORM LETTERS AND TEMPLATES

A **template** or boilerplate is a pattern of words that is used repeatedly. It may be a series of words, phrases, paragraphs, or pages. A **form letter** is a specialized type of template in which only a few phrases or sections vary each time the letter is printed. For example, a contract is a form letter in which the name, address, and some clauses would change for each client. There are two ways to use form letters.

Merge Documents

The most common use of form letters is to **merge** or copy names from a mailing list into a master document, thus producing an individualized document for each name on the original mailing list. The merge operation is performed at print time, so neither the master document nor the mailing list is altered. This type of document is most useful for announcements, bills, or other documents in which the format of the document is consistent but specific pieces of information vary.

Master Documents

Another use of form documents is to create a master document and then to retrieve or copy it each time a new document is needed. The copy is then modified for a particular usage and then saved under a different name. This type of approach is useful when creating contracts, proposals, or other documents that have a common base but which require slightly different text for each use.

Keeping Track of Master Documents

If you use several templates, you should create a LOG document that lists the name and location of each template and summarizes its use. For example:

Name of Document	Location	Usage
Overdue	BILL directory	Merge with CUST60 file
	Billing disk	
LandCtrt	CONTRACTS directory	real estate contract
	Installed hard disk	customize for each use

USING TEMPLATES TO CUSTOMIZE A LETTER

There are two approaches to using templates. The first procedure given is useful for inserting common phrases or paragraphs into a document, for example, to insert a common closing to a business letter. The second is useful when dealing with a document such as a contract, in which you need to make specific changes to a form letter.

Inserting Commonly Used Phrases into a Document

1. Create the master document that contains the phrase, paragraph, or page that you wish to copy.

   Note: It is recommended that the document be given a descriptive name that is easy to remember.

2. Use the Exit (F7) function to save the document and clear the screen. (Do not exit WordPerfect.)

3. List the document in your master document log.

4. Begin entering the customized document. When you are ready to insert the master document wording into the current document, proceed to the next step.

5. Hold down the SHIFT key and press F10 to retrieve a copy of the master document.

6. Enter the name of the master document and press RETURN.

The master document will be copied into the current document at the cursor location.

7. Continue typing the letter.
8. Repeat steps 4 through 7 until the end of the document is reached.
9. Press F10 to save the document.

    The prompt *Document to be Saved* will appear, followed by the name of the last document that was retrieved.

10. Enter a new name. Press RETURN.

    Warning: The document name must be changed. Otherwise, the generic version of the master document will be replaced with a customized version.

Creating Customized Documents from a Master Document

The following procedures describe how to create a master document and then modify it to meet a specific need.

Creating the Master Document

This procedure is performed only once for each master document.

1. Create the master document that contains the information that you wish to copy. When you encounter a word or phrase that is to be replaced with more specific information, such as a name, precede the word with a special character, such as an ampersand (&).

    For example: Regarding the sale of the property at &location.

2. Press F7 to use the Exit function to save the document and clear the screen.

    Note: Use a meaningful name that is easy to remember.

3. Enter the name of the master document into your Master Document Log.

Customizing the Master Document

When the master document was created, a special character was inserted in front of each commonly replaced item. You will now locate each occurrence of this character and adjust the document as appropriate. This procedure is executed each time a copy of the master wording is needed.

1. Hold down the SHIFT key and press F10 to use the Retrieve function.
2. Enter the name of the master document and press RETURN.

The master document will be copied into the current document at the cursor location.

3. Press F2 to select the Search function.

   The prompt *Srch:* will appear.

4. Enter the special character that precedes each item to be modified. For example, press & (ampersand).

   Caution: Do not press RETURN.

5. Press F2 to begin the search.

   The first phrase to be changed will appear.

6. Adjust the text as necessary. For example, replace "&location" with "the property at the northwest corner of ...".

7. Repeat steps 3 through 6 until the end of the document is reached or a *Not Found* message appears.

8. Press F10 to save the document.

   The prompt *Document to be Saved* will appear followed by the name of the last document retrieved.

9. Type the name to be assigned to this document. Press RETURN.

   Warning: A new name must be given to this document. Otherwise, the generic version of the master document will be replaced with a customized version.

USING THE MERGE FACILITY

The easiest way to insert the same type of information into many letters is to create two documents.

- The first or **primary** document contains the form letter or master document. This document consists of a combination of text and merge codes. The text remains the same (constant) each time the document is used. The merge codes tell WordPerfect where to insert the information that varies from one document to the next. They also tell where to find the needed information and when to start and stop the merge process. When naming this document, give the name an extension of **.PF** to make it easy to identify, for example, CONTRACT.PF.

- The second or **secondary** document contains the **data** or information that is to be inserted into the form letter. For example, if you were sending a letter to each salesperson reporting on their status, the secondary document would contain the name, address, quota, and sales figures for each salesperson. Special merge codes are used to identify and separate each piece of information. One code, Merge R (^R), marks the end of a fact or field such as a name, an address, or a sales figure. Another, Merge E (^E), indicates that all of the facts related to one item have been entered, for example, all of the sales information for one salesperson. A group of related facts is called a record. For example, a record could contain a name, street address, city, and phone number. The Merge E (^E) code is used to mark the end of each record. When naming this document, give it an extension of **.SF** to make it easy to identify, for example, SALES.SF.

If the document needs to be in a specific sequence, the Sort function described later in this section can be used to arrange the items into the proper sequence.

Once the format of the primary and the secondary documents is determined to be correct, use the Merge function to combine the information in them. If supplemental information is required that is not in either document, special merge codes permit the entry of additional information at the time the Merge is executed.

The Merge function combines all of this information and produces a customized document for each entry in the secondary document. In the above example, a separate letter would be produced for each sales person. The Merge function does not modify either the primary or the secondary document, so the documents may be reused as often as needed.

Merge Codes

A menu of merge codes is displayed whenever you hold down the ALT key and press F9. The menu will contain all of the codes listed on the next page except for the ^E code, which is accessed by holding down the SHIFT key and pressing F9, and the ^R codes, which are activated by pressing F9.

Merge Code	Meaning
^C	Wait for an entry (response) from the keyboard.
^D	Inserts the current date (the date entered when the system is booted or by issuing and responding to the DOS date command).
^E	Stops the merge when used in the primary document. Marks the end of a record when used in the secondary document.
^F	Identifies the number of the field to be copied from the secondary document and inserted into the primary document. For example, at merge time an ^F1^/ in the primary document is replaced with the value of the first field in the secondary document.
^G	Starts the named macro when the merge is completed. For example, entering ^GBILL will cause the BILL macro to execute at the end of the merge.
^N	Locates and uses the next record in the secondary document. If there are no more records, it ends the merge.
^O	Indicates the beginning and ending of a message to be displayed on the screen. For example, ^O Enter a city name:^O displays the message "Enter a city name"
^P	Names the primary file to be used. To change the file, the format is ^P filename^P. For example, ^P BILLING^P If no document is named (^P^P), the primary document is inserted.
^Q	Stops the merge process.
^R	Marks the end of a field or piece of information
^S	Merges the named secondary file into the document. The format is ^S filename ^S. For example, ^S CLIENT^S changes the secondary file to the CLIENT file.
^T	Sends all text that has been merged to the printer.
^U	Updates (rewrites) the screen.
^V	Copies merge codes into the document being created.

Merge Code Combinations

^N^P^P suppresses automatic page breaks (used for list creation).
^Omessage^O^C displays a message and waits for a response.
^T^N^P^P merges to the printer instead of the screen.

Entering Merge Codes

Merge codes are entered in a document at the location where the code is to take effect. The two ways to insert merge codes are described below.

Using the Merge Code Menu

This method can be used to enter any code except for ^R, which is entered by pressing F9, and ^E, which is entered by holding down the SHIFT key and pressing F9.

1. Position the cursor at the location where the merge code is to be inserted.
2. Hold down the ALT key and press F9.

   A menu displaying all merge codes (except ^R and ^E) will be displayed at the bottom of the screen.

3. Press the letter assigned to the desired merge code. For example, press D to select the ^D code.

   The code will be inserted in the document.

Using the CTRL Key to Enter Merge Codes

This method should not be used to enter the ^F code. If it is, the results of the merge may surprise you.

1. Position the cursor at the location where the code is to be inserted.
2. Hold down the CTRL key and press the letter representing the desired merge code. For example, hold down the CTRL key and press D once to select the ^D code.

   The code will be inserted in the document.

Creating a Primary Document

1. Enter the text of the document.
2. Enter the merge code ^D where the current date is to be inserted.
3. Where information is to be copied from the secondary document:

   a) Hold down the ALT key and press F9 to display the merge codes.

   b) Enter this: F

   The prompt *Field Number?* will appear.

   c) Enter the number that identifies the field. Press RETURN.

Note 1: Fields always appear in the same sequence in a record. For example, if Name is the first field in a record, enter a 1 wherever Name is to be inserted into the document. If the city is the third entry in the record, enter a 3 wherever the city is to be inserted.

Note 2: A field may be used as many times as desired within a document. For example, to enter the name twice, enter F1 twice.

Note 3: Fields do not have to be used in the same sequence as they appear in the secondary document. For example, City (field 3) could be inserted before Name (field 1) was.

Note 4: The primary document need not reference every field in the secondary document. For example, the phone number could be present in the secondary document and omitted in the primary document.

4. Repeat steps 1 through 3 until the document is complete.
5. Press F7 to save the file and clear the screen.
6. Enter Y to save the document.
7. Enter the name of the document and press RETURN.

    Note: To remember that this is a primary document, use an extension of .PF, for example, LETTER1.PF.

8. Press RETURN or type N to clear the screen.

A Sample Primary Document

The sample document below will generate a customized letter for each record on the secondary file. The current date will print at the top of each page where the ^D appears.

```
                              ^D


Dear ^F1^,

We are currently updating our club membership directory.
Please confirm that the addressing information listed below
is correct. If your address is incorrect, please notify me.

          Your name is: ^F1^
          Your street address is: ^F2^
          Your phone number is:    ^F3^

Sincerely yours,
Joe Crossfoot
```

Creating a Data File/Secondary Document

Merge Codes Used in the Secondary Document

^E (Merge E) marks the end of a record or group of related information.
^R (Merge R) marks the end of a field or piece of information.

Rules to Remember When Building a Data File

A data file or secondary document contains the information that varies from one document to the next. The same secondary document may be used with several primary documents.

When building a data file, there are four rules that must be followed.

- Fields are identified by their sequence in the record. Therefore, fields must always appear in the same sequence in each record. For example, if Name is the first field in the first record, it must be the first field in every record in the file.
- A Merge R (F9) code is used to indicate the end of a field. WordPerfect internally assigns a number to the field when it encounters this code. The first field would be identified as field 1, the second as field 2, etc. This permits you to refer to fields by their number.
- There must be the same number of facts in each record. If there is no value or data for a field in a particular record, you must enter a Merge R code to hold its place. For example, if the phone number is not known, enter a Merge R code to indicate that the phone field is empty. If you forget to do this, WordPerfect may insert the wrong field into the primary document, since it identifies each field by its position in the record.
- A Merge E (SHIFT and F9) must be entered at the end of each record. The number of records in a file is limited only by the capacity of your computer.

A Sample Secondary Document

Two records from a sample document are shown below. Each contains a name, street address, and phone number.

Mary McGillity ^R
364 Main Street ^R
312-121-5555 ^R
^E
Sam Spader ^R
101 North Blvd ^R
815-222-8888 ^R
^E

Building the Secondary Document/Data File

1. Enter the value of the first field in the record.
2. Press F9 to insert a Merge R (Merge, Return).
3. Enter the value of the next field in the record.

   If the field is empty, proceed to the next step.

4. Press F9 to mark the end of the field with a Merge R (^R).

   Warning: Do NOT press RETURN after pressing F9.

5. Repeat steps 3 and 4 until each field in the record has been entered.
6. Verify that there is one Merge R code for each field in the record.
7. Hold down the SHIFT key and press F9 to insert a Merge E end-of-record marker.

   The cursor will be positioned at the beginning of the next line.

8. Repeat steps 1 through 7 for each record in the document.
9. Verify that each record contains the same number of fields.
10. Press F7 to save the file and clear the screen.
11. Type Y when the Save prompt appears.
12. Enter the name to be assigned to the file. Press RETURN.

    Note: To remember that this is a secondary file, use an extension of .SF, for example: ADDRESS.SF

13. Press RETURN or type N when the Exit prompt appears.

Creating a File That Prompts for Information to Be Merged

This procedure is commonly used to insert variable information into the primary or secondary document from the keyboard. It can also be used to create a document in which all of the variable information is entered from the keyboard.

If the ^C command is omitted, the procedure can also be used to display informational messages, for example, to tell the person using a procedure that the merge process has begun, to display the name of the customer being processed, to thank someone for entering input.

Note: Information entered from the keyboard can be used to replace or supplement the information on a secondary file.

1. Position the cursor at the location where the merge process should halt and request information.
2. Hold down the CTRL key and press O (^O) to indicate the beginning of

a message. (The O stands for output to the screen.)

3. Enter the prompt that is to appear on the screen when the merge is executed.

   Example: ^O Please enter the first name ^O.

4. Hold down the CTRL key and press O to indicate the end of a message.
5. Hold down the CTRL key and press C (^C) to cause the merge to stop until a response is entered. (The C stands for console, which is an alternate form of keyboard on some computers.)

   Warning: If you forget to do this, it is impossible to respond to the prompt.

   Note: Step 5 may be omitted if your prompt is for information only, for example, ^O Billing Merge In Process ^O.

6. Repeat steps 1 through 5 until each message that is to be displayed during the merge is entered.

   The messages may appear anywhere in the document.

7. If this is a primary document and a secondary file will not be used, enter ^P^P at the end of the document.

   Note: If this is not done, the message can be displayed only once.

8. Press F7 to save the document and clear the screen.
9. Type Y when the Save prompt appears.
10. Enter the name to be assigned the document. Press RETURN.
11. Type N when the Exit prompt appears.

Merging a Form Letter and a Data File

Once the primary and secondary documents are created, the Merge function is used to combine the information in them. Information may also be requested from the keyboard.

Hint: If one record displays and then the merge halts, press F9. It many cases, this will restart the merge process.

1. Clear the screen if necessary by pressing F7 and responding to the prompts.)
2. Hold down the CTRL key and press F9.

   The prompt *1 Merge; 2 Sort; 3 Sorting Sequence* will appear.

3. Type 1 to select Merge.
4. Enter the name of the primary file that contains the form document. Press RETURN.

5. Enter the name of the secondary file that contains the data to be inserted into the form document. Press RETURN.

   Note: If there is no secondary file, press RETURN.

   The prompt *Merging* will appear at the bottom of the screen. When the merge is completed, the customized documents will be displayed on the screen.

6. If a message is displayed that requests information, enter the required information, then immediately press F9 to continue the merge.
7. If this is the first time the documents have been merged, use the cursor movement keys to scroll through the document and verify that the information was inserted correctly.
8. Hold down the SHIFT key and press F7 to print the documents if there are only a few records. Otherwise, use the F7 key to save the printed output.

   Note: If the document format needs to be changed before printing, use F7 to save the file, change the formats, and then print the documents. Otherwise, the default format may be used in error.

Merging a Form Letter with Keyboard Information

Use this procedure if there is no secondary file and all of the variable information is entered from the keyboard.

1. Clear the screen if necessary by pressing F7. (Respond N to the second prompt.)
2. Hold down the CTRL key and press F9.

   The prompt *1 Merge; 2 Sort; 3 Sorting Sequence* will appear.

3. Type 1 to select Merge.
4. Enter the name of the primary file containing the form document. Press RETURN.
5. Press RETURN when prompted for the name of the secondary file.

   The prompt *Merging* will appear at the bottom of the screen. When the merge is completed, the customized documents will be displayed on the screen.

   A message requesting information will be displayed.

6. Enter the requested information.

   Caution: Once the information is entered, immediately proceed to the next step. Otherwise, the merge may terminate.

7. Press F9 to continue the merge.

   If the merge message does not appear and more prompts are expected, verify the ^P^P is entered at the end of the master document.

8. Use the F7 key to save the merged output. The output may then be retrieved, formatted, and printed at your convenience.

   If there are not a large number of records, the print command may be used to immediately print the output.

Merging to the Printer

If you do not wish to display the customized documents on the screen before you print them, execute this procedure before merging the documents.

1. Position the cursor at the end of the primary document, that is, immediately after the closing sentence or phrase.
2. Hold down the CTRL key and press T to cause the document to be "typed" on the printer. (It is then erased from memory.)
3. Hold down the CTRL key and press N to tell WordPerfect to find the next record.

   Note: If there are no more records, the merge will end.

   Warning: If this command is not entered, only one record will be printed.

4. Hold down the CTRL key and press P twice to indicate that the primary document is to be used.
5. Press F10 to save the changes.

Stopping a Merge

1. Press F1 to cancel the merge.

Restarting a Merge

This procedure will work only if the merge has halted as a result of a Merge command and unexpected keys, such as an extra RETURN, have not been pressed.

1. Press F9.

Printing Mailing Labels

The steps in printing mailing labels are:

1. create the primary file, as described in *Creating a Primary Document*;
2. create the secondary file, as described in *Creating a Secondary Document*;
3. merge the two files, as in *Merging a Form Letter and a Data File*;
4. use F7 to save the print output;
5. retrieve the Print file;
6. change the page format to the correct label size by using the Page (ALT F8) and Line (SHIFT F8) Format menus.

    Note: If you are using 2-by-4 inch labels, use the following Page and Line format values:

    | Form length | 12 |
    | Page length | 9 |
    | Top margin | 6 |
    | Left margin | 5 |
    | Right margin | 35 |

7. print the labels using the SHIFT F7 command.

Linking Several Documents or Templates Together

1. Create one document for each sentence, paragraph, page, or group of pages that you wish to link together.

    For example, if you are composing a contract, the documents might be: opening, clause1, clause2, clause3, closing.

    Note: Merge codes do not need to be present in these document unless you wish to access information in a secondary file.

2. Use the F7 key to clear the screen.
3. Hold down the CTRL key and press P.
4. Enter the name of the first document to be printed.
5. Hold down the CTRL key and press P.
6. Press RETURN to advance to the next line.
7. Repeat steps 3 through 6 for each document to be combined.

    Note: List the documents in the order that they are to be printed.

8. Press F7 to save the file and clear the screen.
9. Enter Y to the Save prompt.
10. Enter the name of the file to be saved.
11. Enter N to the Exit prompt.
12. If you do not wish the document to be displayed on the screen, follow the procedure *Merging to the Printer*.

13. To produce a printed document, follow the procedure *Merging a Form Letter and a Data File.*

SORTING INFORMATION

The WordPerfect Sort command can be used to sort individual words, columns, lines, or paragraphs. It also can be used to sort a block of text.

The sort operation consists of two separate procedures. In the first procedure, you identify the document to be sorted. In the second, you describe the type of sort that you wish to perform and the information to be sorted.

Caution: When sorting a document that you are currently editing, save the document before beginning the sort procedure. Otherwise, if you make an error, it will be difficult to reconstruct the original document.

Selecting the Sort Function

In this step you identify the document to be sorted.
1. Use the F7 command to clear the screen if it is not already clear.
2. Hold down the SHIFT key and press F10 to retrieve a document.
3. Enter the name of the document that you wish to sort.
4. Hold down the CTRL key and press F9.

   1 Merge; 2 Sort; 3 Sorting Sequence will appear at the bottom of the screen.

5. Type 2 to select Sort.
6. Press RETURN to select the current document.

   If you have changed your mind, enter the name of the document that you wish to sort; then press RETURN.

7a. To replace the text in the current document with the sorted text:

   a) Press RETURN.

   A prompt will be displayed, asking you to confirm that you wish to replace the current document.

   b) Enter a Y

7b. To store the sorted text in another document:

   a) Enter the name of the document that will contain the sorted information.

   b) Press RETURN.

The Sort/Select Display will appear on the screen.

8. Proceed to the procedure *Using the Sort/Select Display.*

Sorting a Block of Text

1. Hold down the ALT key and press F4 to invoke the block command.
2. Use the cursor movement keys to mark the block of text to be sorted.
3. Hold down the CTRL key and press F9.

    The Sort/Select Display will appear on the screen.

4. Select the type of sort to be executed, using the *Sort/Select Display* procedure that follows.

    The sorted text will replace the original text.

Using the Sort/Select Display to Describe the Sort

When you enter the Sort/Select Display, the current file is displayed on the top ten lines of the screen. The bottom half of the screen contains the Sort/Select menu. The two parts of the screen are separated by a ruler line.

The Sort/Select Screen

The first line on the Sort/Select Display names the last type of sort that was executed, for example, sort by line. The next group of lines show the current key settings. Then a line is displayed that describes the type of action being performed. For example:

Action	Order	Type of Sort
Sort	Ascending	Line Sort

The bottom line contains a menu of possible activities. The choices are:

1. Perform action	Performs the action listed in the first column.
2. View	Displays a different part of the current document.
3. Keys	Identifies the fields used to sequence the report. For example, if the primary sort key is Name, the text is placed in order by name.
4. Select	identifies selection criteria for the sort. For example: select all names beginning with A.

5. Action   Changes the action being performed.
6. Order   Changes the sort order. Possible choices
             are Ascending or Descending. If ascending
             is selected, the items are sequenced so that
             the smallest item is displayed first and
             and the largest item are last, for example,
             1 2 3. If descending is selected, the items
             will be sequenced so that the largest item is
             displayed first and the smallest item is last,
             for example, 3 2 1.
7. Type   Used to change the sort type, for example,
             Line, paragraph, secondary merge.

Sorting by a Line Item

The Line sort is used to place each line in sequence based on a field or key, which you provide. Line sorts are usually used with documents that are organized into rows and columns, such as address files. For example, the Line sort could be used to arrange an address file in last-name sequence.

1. If Line sort does not appear at the top of the screen, press 7 to select the type option, then press 2 to select *Line*.

2. Press 3 to select keys.

   The cursor will move to under the heading *Typ*.

3. Enter N (for numeric) if the field you are sorting on contains numbers. (The field may also contain commas, periods, and dollar signs.)

   Enter A (for alphanumeric) if the field contains letters or a mixture of letters and numbers. If the field contains only numbers, the numbers must all be the same length, for example, zipcodes.

   The cursor will move to the Field column.

4. Enter the number of the field containing the sort key.

   Example: If you are sorting an address file in name sequence and Name is the first item in the line, enter a 1.

5. To sort a document on a particular word within the field, such as last name, enter the position that the word occupies within the field. Since many fields consist of only one word, the default is 1.

   Example: To sort on the second word in the field, enter a 2.

   The field number is established at the time the file is defined. See *Creating a Data File/Secondary Document* for more information.

6. Press RETURN.

7. Press F7 to return to the menu.
8. Press 6 if you wish to change the sort order.

    Then press 1 to select ascending order or 2 to select descending order.
9. Press 1 to sort the document.

Document Filing and Housekeeping

THE DOCUMENT DIRECTORY

The document directory is a list of all of the files in the directory. Many of the procedures in this section begin by pressing F5 to view the names of the documents in the current directory. The next three procedures explain how to access the current directory, change the directory if desired, search the directory for a specific document and then leave the directory. Unless otherwise specified, the other procedures in this section are executed from the directory display.

ACCESSING OR CHANGING THE DIRECTORY

This procedure can be used to access, change or create a directory. You may also change directories by typing an equal sign (=) when the current directory prompt appears.

1. Press F5.

    The current directory will be displayed.

2. Press RETURN to see a list of documents on the current directory.

    When the list of documents appears, execute the next step if you wish to

101

change directories.

3. Press 7 to select Change Directory.

   The prompt *New Directory* = followed by the name of the current directory will appear.

4. Type the drive to be used next, for example, B:
5. Type a backslash (\) followed by the name of the directory to which you wish to switch, for example, \ billing. Press RETURN.

   Note: This may be a new or existing directory.

   The prompt *Create* directory name? *(Y/N) N* will appear where directory name is the name entered above.

6. Type Y to create a new directory.

   Press RETURN to switch to an existing directory.

   The directory will become the current directory. To return to the original directory, repeat this procedure, but enter the name of the original directory in step 5.

Locating a Document Name

You can also use the cursor movement keys (arrows, plus and minus signs, etc) to proceed to the document.

1. Type the first letter in the name of the document.

   The prompt *Name Search. Use space or arrows to reset* appears at the bottom of the screen, and the cursor jumps to the first document beginning with the letter typed.

2. Use the cursor movement keys to move to the desired document name or type the next letter in the name.

   Repeat step 2 until the desired name is highlighted.

3. Press the spacebar (if necessary) to display the menu at the bottom of the screen.

Leaving the Document Directory
Version 4.1

1. Press RETURN to exit the directory listing and return to the current document.

Version 4.2

1a. Press 0 or F7 to return to the current document.

Pressing RETURN causes you to return to the directory prompt and view the name of the active directory.

COPYING A DOCUMENT

This procedure can be used to copy documents from one disk or directory to another, as well as to copy documents within a directory. It assumes that you have already used the appropriate procedures to access the directory listing and position the cursor on the document to be copied.

1. Position the cursor on the name of the document to be copied.
2. Press 8 to select *Copy* from the directory menu.

   The prompt *Copy this file to:* will appear.
3. To copy the document to another drive, enter the name of the drive, for example C:
4. To copy the document to another directory, enter a backslash (\) followed by the name of the directory, for example, \ directoryname.
5. Enter the name to be assigned to the new copy of the document.

   Note: When copying the document into another directory, precede the name with a backslash.
6. Press RETURN.

   The document whose name is highlighted will be copied.

DELETING A DOCUMENT

1. Position the cursor on the name of the directory document to be erased.
2. Press 2 to select *Delete* from the directory menu.

   The prompt *Delete* document name?-(*Y/N*) *N* will appear.
3. Press Y to delete the named document or RETURN to change your mind.

   The document will be erased.

BROWSING/LOOKING AT A DOCUMENT

This procedure can be used to quickly enter and examine a document. It cannot be used to modify a document.

1. Position the cursor on the name of the document to be examined.
2. Press 6 to select *Look* from the directory menu.

    The first page of the document will appear.

3. Press the down arrow, plus (+), or PgDn keys to proceed through the document.
4. Press RETURN to leave the document and return to the list of documents.

LOCATING DOCUMENTS THAT CONTAIN SPECIFIC WORDS

This procedure is used to locate the names of all documents which contain a particular word or phrase. The search does not distinguish between upper and lower case characters.

Rules governing the search are listed below.

- The word or phrase may contain up to 20 characters, including punctuation marks.
- To search for all words with a common base, type the desired characters, and then type an * to indicate that you want to match any character or series of characters.

For example, to find all documents containing the word pattern "DOC", enter "DOC*". This will locate documents containing the words document, doctor, dock, or any other word that begins with doc. If "doc*r" was entered, WordPerfect would locate doctor, doctaer, docr, etc.

- A question mark will match any single character. So the word pattern "D?C' will match doc, dic, dac.
- If the phrase contains a space, comma, semicolon, or quotation mark, enclose the phrase in quotation marks, for example: "heart of the city".
- To locate documents that contain two or more phrases, list the phrases to be located and separate them with a semicolon or a space. The space acts as a logical AND.

For example, to locate documents which contain both of the phrases "the first" and "the third", type *"the first" "the third"*.

- To find a document that contains either phrase 1 OR phrase 2, separate the phrases by a comma. The comma acts like a logical OR. A document will be selected if it contains either of the two phrases or words named.

For example, to locate all documents containing either the word WordPerfect or the word Lotus 1-2-3, enter the word pattern *"WordPerfect", "Lotus 1-2-3"*.

1. Press 9 to select *Word Search* from the directory menu.

    The prompt *Word Pattern:* will appear.

2. Enter the word or phrase to be located; press RETURN to begin the search.

    Note: The search may take a long time if there are many files in the directory.

3. The complete directory listing will be replaced with a list of documents that contain the desired words or phrases.
4. Position the cursor on the name of the document that you wish to work with next.
5. Enter the number of the action to be performed next. For example, press 1 to retrieve the highlighted document.

PRINTING A DOCUMENT

This procedure may be used as an alternative to the print procedures controlled by the SHIFT F7 keys. Since the printer menu will not be displayed, this procedure should not be used if you need to temporarily change the printer assignment or number of copies. It is recommended that you let one document complete printing before selecting another for print.

1. Position the cursor on the name of the document to be printed.
2. Press 4 to select *Print* on the directory menu.

    The screen will blink. As soon as the printer is free, the document will be printed.

RENAMING A DOCUMENT

1. Position the cursor on the name that is to be changed.
2. Press 3 to select *Rename* on the directory menu.

The prompt *New Name:* will appear.

3. Enter the new name to be assigned to the document.
4. Press RETURN.

The document will be renamed.

RETRIEVING A DOCUMENT FROM THE DIRECTORY

When a document is retrieved, it is copied from the disk and inserted into the current document at the current cursor location.

1. Position the cursor on the name of the document to be retrieved.
2. Press 1 to select *Retrieve* on the directory manu.

The current document will be displayed.

RETRIEVING A NON-WORDPERFECT DOCUMENT FROM THE DIRECTORY

Warning: The Text-In function must be used to retrieve files that are not in WordPerfect format. Otherwise, the screen may lock when you try to page through the document.

While this procedure can be used to retrieve files created by WordStar, MultiMate, or other packages, it will not remove all of the codes that those packages insert. Instead, to fully convert the files, insert the learning diskette in drive A, type Convert, and then follow the prompts. Then retrieve the converted file.

Note: If the document begins with a margin of zero, reset the left margin from 10 to zero before beginning this procedure.

1. Position the cursor on the name of the document to be converted.
2. Press 5 (Text In) to retrieve the document.

The document will be inserted into the current document at the cursor location.

TRANSLATING DOCUMENTS TO AND FROM ASCII

ASCII is a format that can be read by most programs. To convert the document to ASCII, WordPerfect removes most of the codes that are displayed when the Reveal Codes key combination is pressed. (ALT F3).

Warning: The Tab code (9) and hard page break code (12) RETURN codes are retained. Two codes will be placed at the end of a line to generate a hard RETURN. The first, 13, causes a carriage return. The second, 10, generates a line feed. If your program does not require both of these codes, use an editor or write a program to remove them.

To convert a WordPerfect document to a format used by a specific program, return to DOS, insert the Learning diskette in drive A: and type Convert.

Using the Text-In/Out Function to Translate Documents

1. Hold down the CTRL key and press F5.

    A menu of options will appear.

To save the current document as an ASCII file

2. Press 1 (*Save current document as a DOS text file.*)

    The prompt *Document to be Saved* will appear followed by the name of the current document.

3. Enter a new name to save the converted file as another document. Press RETURN.

    Warning: If a new name is not entered, the original document will be replaced by the converted version of the document.

    The document will be converted and stored on the disk.

To retrieve an ASCII file

2. Press 2 (*Retrieve a DOS text file*).

    The prompt *Document to be Retrieved* will appear.

3. Enter the name of the document to be retrieved.
4. Press RETURN.

    The document will be inserted into the current document at the cursor location.

CONVERTING DOCUMENTS INTO OTHER FORMATS

This procedure will translate a file so that it can be edited by WordPerfect. Some of the formats which can be converted include: DCA, DIF, WordStar,

Multimate. MailMerge files from dBase, WordStar and other word processors can be converted to WordPerfect secondary merge files. The procedure can also be used to translate WordPerfect files into formats understood by other packages.

1. Exit WordPerfect.
2. Remove the WordPerfect diskette from drive A:.
3. Insert the Learning diskette in drive A:.
4. Insert the disk containing the document to be converted in drive B.
5. Type Convert from the DOS prompt.
6. Type B: followed by the name of the file to be converted. (Do NOT press RETURN.)
7. Type B: followed by the name to be assigned to the new converted file.

    Note: This must be a different name from the name entered in step 4.

8. Press RETURN.

    Warning: Do not press RETURN when the Title Screen appears. It will be automatically replaced by the next screen.

    A list of conversion format options will appear.

9. Enter the number opposite the format which describes the type of input document being converted. For example, type 1 if the input document is in WordPerfect format.

    A WordPerfect document will be created for choices 2 through 6. Choices 7 and 9 will generate a secondary Merge file. If option 7 (MailMerge) is entered, additional information about the file will be requested.

    A menu of output conversion options will appear.

10. Enter the number opposite the name of the format to be used for the output document.

    The document will be converted.

BACKING UP DOCUMENTS

To prevent loss, documents should be saved at regular intervals. Either press F10 every page or so to save your work or use the timed backup option discussed in the *Defaults* chapter.

RESTORING A BACKUP DOCUMENT

This procedure can be used to recover backup files when the system has gone down accidentally.

1. Reboot the system and enter WordPerfect.

    This message will appear: *ERROR: Overflow files already exist.* Then the menu below will appear.

    Directory in use! 1 Exit 2 Use Another Directory 3 Overwrite Files:

2. Type 3 to eliminate the overwrite files.
3. Press F5 to view the document directory.

    Dir B: will appear on the screen.

4. Press RETURN to accept the directory displayed, or enter the directory containing your documents.
5. Position the cursor on {WP} BACK.1.

    This document will probably be near the end of the list.

6. Press 3 to rename the document. (Optional)
7. Press 1 to retrieve the document.

    The version of the document which was saved will be retrieved. Any changes made to the document after the last Save was executed must be reentered.

Defaults

THE SET-UP MENU

Several of WordPerfect's defaults may be changed permanently from the Set-up menu. The defaults for line spacing, tabs, margins, justification, screen size, backup options, beep options and which directory or drive the Speller or Thesaurus should be loaded from are options that can be changed by using the Set-up menu. The first procedure in this section tells you how to access and exit this feature. The remaining procedures describe how to modify some of the default values controlled by this menu.

USING THE SET-UP MENU

1. Enter WordPerfect by typing WP/S at the DOS prompt and press the RETURN key.

    The Set-up menu is displayed on screen.

2. Make the appropriate changes to modify WordPerfect options permanently.

3. Type 0 (zero) to enter WordPerfect with newly selected options permanently installed or

111

Press the function key F1 to return to DOS without installing the changed defaults.

Setting the Automatic Backup Using the Set-Up Menu

WordPerfect has two backup features: The Timed Backup and the Original Backup. Either or both features may be installed.

Timed Backup

The Timed Backup feature enables you to recover data that could otherwise be lost because of power failure, computer failure or problems which occur and do not permit you to save work prior to leaving WordPerfect.

The Timed Backup feature interrupts and saves the current Doc 1 file under the name {WP}BACK.1 every *n* minutes as specified by you. The current Doc 2 file, if any, is saved under the name {WP}BACK.2.

The Timed Backup files are closed and erased when you leave WordPerfect using the F7 (exit) key. In the event that you leave WordPerfect due to a power or computer failure, the files are stored on disk and can later be used. To use backup files that have been saved it is necessary to rename the backup file before retrieving it.

Original Backup

Normally the original WordPerfect document is replaced when you save the file. The Original Backup feature saves a copy of the original document each time you update the document. As a result, two versions of the document would exist. The first version would contain your latest changes. The second version, which would have a .BK! extension, would contain an image of your file before you saved it. This type of backup permits you to change your mind if you saved a file and then later discovered that it contained a serious error.

Caution: Be sure that the first eight characters in the file name are unique. Otherwise NAME.DOC and NAME.DAT would both create a backup file named NAME.BK! Since duplicate file names cannot exist, the backup for the last file edited would replace whatever was stored previously.

Installing the Backup Features

1. Type 4 to select the Backup feature of the Set-up menu.

   The prompt *Number of minutes between each backup* will appear.

3. Enter the number of minutes to elapse before the file is saved; press RETURN.

   Note 1: Enter a low enough figure that you do not lose a significant amount of work, but a high enough one that you do not become frustrated by constant interruptions to save the file. A value between 5 and 15 minutes will probably meet your needs.

Note 2: Press F1 (Cancel) to skip the Timed Backup prompts and proceed directly to step 5, Original Backup prompts.

The prompt *Where should timed backup files be stored? Enter the full path name* will appear.

4. Enter the drive and, if appropriate, a path name. Press RETURN.

   Note: Do NOT enter the file name. Doc 1 is assigned a name of {WP}BACK.1. Doc 2 is assigned a name of {WP}BACK.2.

   The cursor will move to the prompt for the original Backup Option: *Back Up the Original Document (Y/N): N*

5. Type Y to backup the original document.

   Press the function key F1 (Cancel key) if you do not wish to create a permanent backup for your documents.

   The Set-up menu will appear.

Changing Formatting Defaults Permanently

The defaults for the Line Format (SHIFT F8), Page Format (ALT and F8), Print Format (CTRL F8), Print (SHIFT F7), Date (SHIFT F5), Insert/Typeover (INS), Mark Text (ALT F5), Footnote (CTRL F7), Repeat (ESC) and Screen (CTRL F3) functions can be permanently changed by using this procedure. (Refer to the chapter *Formatting a Document* if you need more information.)

1. Type 2 to change the formatting defaults from the Set-up menu.

   A menu is displayed on screen listing the keys and the initial settings that can be changed.

2. Press the function key combination which represents the desired function and then select the feature to be changed.

   Example: To turn off right justification:

   a) Hold down the CTRL key and press F8.

   b) Enter 3 to turn off justification.

   c) Press RETURN to return to the Change Initial Settings menu.

3. Press RETURN to return to the Set-up menu.

Changing Screen Size

This option can be used if your monitor is capable of displaying a screen wider than 80 columns and longer than 25 rows.

1. Type 3 to select the Screen size option of the Set-up menu.
2. Enter the new row settings. Press RETURN.
3. Enter the new column settings. Press RETURN.

   The Set-up menu will be displayed.

Changing Drives and/or Directories for Speller and Thesaurus

1. Type 1 to select the Set Directories or Drives option of the Set-up menu.

   You will be requested to enter the drive and/or full path name where the following three files are to be stored:

   Thesaurus (TH.WP); Speller dictionary (LEX.WP); the supplemental dictionary.

3. Respond to each prompt by entering the drive and/or full path name (hard disk users). Press RETURN.

   Warning: Do not enter the name of the file itself.

   After the last response is entered, the Set-up menu is displayed.

Invoking Automatic Backup When Starting WordPerfect

This procedure permits you to save your file at regular intervals without permanently changing the Backup default.

1. Type WP/B-*n* when starting WordPerfect, where *n* is the number of minutes after which the current file is automatically saved.

   The backup feature will automatically back up the current file every *n* minutes of the WordPerfect session.

Invoking WordPerfect Without the Fast Option/Adjusting WordPerfect for TopView and DeskTop Packages

Some compatibles have screens which go blank if you do not enter data during a set interval. If you are using one of these computers, or if you are using a separate windowing or desktop package, you must specify non-flash mode.

1. Type WP/NF when starting WordPerfect.